A SETH BOOK

THE EARLY CLASS SESSIONS

Book 1

by Jane Roberts

Sessions
9/12/67 to 11/25/69

A Note about THE EARLY CLASS SESSIONS & THE SETH AUDIO COLLECTION

The Early Seth Class Session books will consist of Seth class sessions that are different from those published in The Seth Audio Collection and Individual Seth Tapes and CD's. The Audio Collection & CD's cover the Seth class sessions held in Jane Roberts "ESP" class from 1972-1979. The Early Seth Class Session books will cover the earlier Seth class sessions (from 1967 to the end of 1971) for which we have no audio recordings. In addition, some later class sessions for which we have no recordings will also be included in the Early Seth Class Session books.

The Seth audios are actual recordings of Seth speaking during Jane's class in Elmira NY and are available in CD format along with written transcripts. There are 39 CD's currently published and more will be forthcoming.

THE EARLY SESSIONS

The Early Sessions consist of the first 510 sessions dictated by Seth through Jane Roberts. There are 9 books in *The Early Sessions* series.

THE PERSONAL SESSIONS

The Personal Sessions, often referred to as "the deleted sessions," are Seth sessions that Jane Roberts and Rob Butts considered to be of a highly personal nature and were therefore kept in separate notebooks from the main body of the Seth material. *The Personal Sessions* are published in 7 volumes.

NEW AWARENESS NETWORK INC.
P.O. BOX 192, MANHASSET, N.Y. 11030

WWW. SETHCENTER.COM

A SETH BOOK

THE EARLY CLASS SESSIONS

Book 1

by Jane Roberts

Sessions
9/12/67 to 11/25/69

© 2008 by Laurel Lee Davies-Butts

Published by New Awareness Network Inc.

New Awareness Network Inc.
P.O. Box 192
Manhasset, New York 11030

Class member's names used herein are pseudonyms.

Opinions and statements on health and medical matters expressed in this book are those of the author and are not necessarily those of or endorsed by the publisher. Those opinions and statements should not be taken as a substitute for consultation with a duly licensed physician.

Cover Design: Michael Goode
Editorial: Rick Stack
Typography: Raymond Todd, Michael Goode

All rights reserved. This book may not be reproduced in whole or in part, without written permission from the publisher, except by a reviewer who may quote brief passages in a review; nor may any part of this book be reproduced, stored in a retrieval system, or transmitted in any form or by any means electronic, mechanical, photocopying, recording, or other, without written permission from the publisher.

ISBN 978-0-9768978-5-9
Printed in U.S.A.

I dedicate The Early Class Sessions
*to my wife, Jane Roberts,
who lived her 55 years
with the greatest creativity
and the most valiant courage.*

-Robert F. Butts, Jr.

SESSION 363, ESP CLASS,
SEPTEMBER 12, 1967 8:45 PM TUESDAY

(This session was held for three of Jane's students. Attending were Florence McIntyre, Sally Benson, and Rachel Clayton.

(It was hoped that in this session Seth would give impressions concerning the Gallaghers' vacation.

Good evening.

("Good evening, Seth.")

My heartiest wishes to all here present. Now, we will speak for a brief time on some general matters while we make preparations for the Gallagher material.

Now, all of you in this room know but a small portion of your whole inner self. This inner self of yours, however, knows you well and guides your actions whether or not you intellectually realize its presence.

We will, at one time or another, speak with you each in a more private session. For now I simply greet you. Joseph, give us a moment if you please.

([Rob:] "Yes.")

These are impressions dealing with the Gallaghers. Arcadia. A name—a name of a place that means low valley in English. A native who is dressed in clothes that do not belong to him: he is performing. The clothes are a costume from another culture.

An A here. A boat. The Gallaghers are on a boat. They pass three islands and land on the fourth. There is something spilled on the boat, and a scramble.

A strange fruit they see, it resembles a coconut but it is not one. It has pink pulp.

A party of four on the boat. The initials M, B or M, D and a child of six. An initial encounter that is not pleasant. Someone screams: possibly a child involved.

The Jesuit notices a three-legged dog. He wanders far off from the others, the Jesuit. *(Note: The Jesuit is Seth's nickname for Bill Granger.)*

There is a plane down or a ship in difficulty in their locality and resulting activity in a port at the far tip end of the island furthest down in this particular group of islands *(voice slurred and slow)*. Perhaps planes sent out from the port to search. The initials T, B, A, here somewhere connected. The port at this island seems to be the only main town. *(Voice slow, slurred, long pauses.)*

While we are dealing with this, there is unusual activity around Cape Hope and this is connected with what has happened. *(Mouths words first.)* There is a town or island or bay, some area in the vicinity that sounds like Balinda. This is not it, however.

Baly–Winda... Baly Wanda...

Now more personally our friend, the Jesuit. There is a large wooden object that he is taken with, like a totem, fatter it seems though and not so tall as one. He speaks with several male natives and an American man, from Minnesota, who deals in a business that is connected with salt.

(Voice very slow and slurred all through here and many pauses.)

SESSION 363

An engagement between 4 and 5 today. And loud noises that are music. Two flags on one island and an administration building that is orange or pink. They eat or talk with a man *(voice very faint)* whose name has to do with grip, you see, as bag or valise. Do you see?

([Rob:] "Yes.")

Some point over the spending of nine dollars in particular, a five and four ones, something outrageously priced.

A visit, a settlement of thatched or straw covered huts, nine to twelve of these. Our friend sees a shaman. A particular walk through a jungle area. Our friend, the Jesuit, is here, and five others have gone this same way earlier and he knows this: it is his reason for going, you see.

He and the Catlover *(Seth's nickname for Maggie Granger)* chose one particular way because they are too cagey and shrewd to take another recommended way. Now one place they stay: has water on one side and foliage on the other with large square openings in the front; and I do not believe here by the large square openings there is any glass. The steps are from the side, three or four. They find this place on their own. Someone has hung clothing on a line though beside the place. They can stand and look out over the ocean and sight two or three other islands, one they have visited. They plan to see three other islands.

Now you may take your break or end the session as you prefer.

([Rob:] "We'll take a short break."

(9:10. Break. Jane didn't seem to be aware that her manner had been very detached, dreamy. She "saw" some of the surroundings but had no real projection.)

(9:20. Resume.)

Now a rather odd connection with Grumbacher, or painting supplies, for the Grangers.

They meet a man in a hut-like place. He is thin, with a white shirt that is not fully buttoned. He does not have a beard but his face is prickly and dark. He smokes and his fingers are long and stained with nicotine. His trousers are somehow strange, and he wears white shoes or not shoes, but his feet appear lighter, you see. There is a light behind him also and he stands at a partially opened door, and our friend the Jesuit speaks to him. There is an identical structure very close by, perhaps attached, you see. There are steps and men sit on them. The stranger lives on the island and he wears a ring. He may also have on other jewelry.

The Catlover stands on the ground, waiting, and this structure is also facing the water. There is an S connected with the stranger, also an A. And the Grangers have come from down a road or path, that is somewhat hilly, from a settlement there, and they have been riding, perhaps bicycles or wagon-like vehicles—or a wagon driven by animals—pulled by animals.

There is a church that has burned down and the place is known for an uprising that occurred years earlier.

We are not sure here, the name brings to mind the

name of Sacramento, though again this is not the precise name.

A strange building there built in 1924. It does not really belong there. There are no others like it and it contains records that have an historical connection and the records come from another place, another country.

Strongly I have the number 5. Some event at 5 today, however, that will stick in their minds when they return.

Now the grass is growing here but it is turning brown. There is a brown high grass in this one area and the bottom of the trees is black and there are large berries. This is a particular area, a waste area, that has been somehow ravaged and perhaps, once burned, you see. It is ringed in by trees and the historical and psychic connections there are not good, having to do with sacrifices. Monchuco *(Rob's interpretation)—the* Monchuco. (*My interpretation is that two words may have been meant; more like Monchu chu? Mon choo choo?*)

The Monchuco were here and worshipped a half-bull, half-woman deity and the bull was a black one and sacrifices were thrown into the sea. There is this spot where a thatched temple once stood and in a more distant past a connection, strange as it may seem, with an offshoot of the Inca civilization. This spot is on the third island and this island itself will be involved in a disaster within a short time. It will be, to all intent and purposes, wiped out.

A former governor of another country once stayed at

this island also and he was removed from office ahead of schedule or otherwise politically ruined, returning to his homeland in disgrace.

Now we are returning here and we shall close this evening's session. My heartiest wishes to you all.

(9:40 PM. This was an odd session. Jane didn't sound like Seth at all a good part of the time, and she realized this to some degree. She felt as if she were projecting through time, rather than through space at the last; re: Seth's moment points. Perhaps Jane was speaking more for herself with Seth's guidance. She started with the Seth voice then gradually used one that was between her normal voice and Seth's. Florence noticed that the tense changed from we to I for a while also.)

SECOND PART OF SESSION, TUESDAY, SEPTEMBER 12, 1967

(This portion is typed up by Jane Butts from notes taken on the spot by Robert Butts.

(After the end of the Seth session, I suddenly got the impression of a name, Martha. I hesitated, then asked if the name meant anything to anyone in the room; I was sure it did. Florence said that her sister-in-law's name was Martha. Then I asked if Grandview had anything to do with Martha. Florence said that Martha had lived on Grand Island in Buffalo. With the assurance that this was correct, I went into a trance to see what impressions I could get for the students. When I was finished the results were discussed by the students;

SESSION 9/12/1967

they told me what impressions were hits, etc. Apparently about 90% of the impressions were correct.

(The impressions will be given with a note as to their accuracy.)

I have a connection with Martha and water, perhaps because you told me she lived on Grand Island, or perhaps this is an indication of a street name such as Lake Ave, Water St., etc.

A house with pine trees, back kitchen. *(Yes to both; Martha's house.)* Two children. *(Yes, Martha's.)* A girl with curly brown hair. *(Yes.)* Name like Anna or Annette or Anita. *(Name is Alice.)* Boy or girl about 6th grade. *(No.)* The man, business, bottles or coverings, containers. *(?)*

An earlier association further west than Buffalo, several states further west than New York State.

(Yes. Leaving room to fill in information here) The name Francis, male or female.

(Yes, Florence has a female cousin by that name.)

Scheduled events included service. *(Yes, Martha's husband was in the service.)* Air Force before it was the Air Force. *(No.)*

A history major or deep interest in the past, a hobby of the past. *(?)*

Originally five in the family. *(No.)*

A woman in the background with a connection with Winchester... Rochester? Rochester or Winchester... fairly elderly. May have been a Grandmother, possibly now dead.

(Most interesting. This did not apply to Florence, but to

Rachel. Her present employer's wife has white hair, but is young. She lived both in Rochester and Winchester.)

The impression of four stars, service? Not sure. *(?)*

A collection of paraphernalia in one place connected with business or hobby perhaps, in basement, strong connection with guns.

(Yes. Martha's husband, Florence's brother, lost his life as a result of war wounds. Martha keeps all his possessions together, including his guns and rifles.)

A lease and four years connected with it, a new location. *(?)*

I'm jumping now to an uncle of Sally's: with a mustache and with an old photo. This means he is now an old man now or is dead. The fashion of his clothes is old. First a black mustache and then it turns white. He wears a uniform of some sort or fancy clothes, a hat that is strange.

(Yes. All of this describes a photograph of Sally's grandfather—not uncle; a photo she has not seen until approximately four days before this session.)

A European connection... name, Alfred... last name beginning with an S and has several F's. Not right. Sinorfis or something like that.

(Yes. Am leaving room for correct information.
(Schachter—his name.
([MD]This was handwritten on page—as if added later.)

Perhaps on mother's side, a relative or great uncle, name Grayfus? *(?)*

And another man, younger, light skin, wears light colored trousers, part of uniform? Worn in work? With stripes? At the time he seems to be 34 but he is older now. Two children and one a male. Previous marriage. Sally's husband past.

(Sally said this described her husband who has married again. He wore light blue trousers at their marriage. Leaving room to get more information.)

Now sandy hair. Connection with someone—Edward. And an A, with a large family and a particular picture of the family, old, three girls with large hair ribbons, two boys, several years older, picture taken on porch steps very early 1900's. Perhaps in a city B or the name begins with B. And a sister, a career woman before this was general practice.

(? Sally said yes to some of this. Leaving room here.)

Now, Rachel: A rather early illness, of years, I believe.

(Yes. Ruth had TB and was very ill.)

I get Anna again, mentioned earlier in connection with Florence, does this belong to Rachel instead? *(?)*

A sister. *(?)*

Seems a doctor was a close friend or had a strong effect on your life.

(Yes. The doctor who tended her was an old family friend, knew both the father and son, both doctors.) Two brothers. *(?)*

A mother who... dropped dead at 35, or something happened drastically to change her. No, died at #35; or had a psychological tragedy, seems to be Rachel's mother.

(Yes. Rachel's mother died at 35, shortly after giving

birth to Rachel.) Also home in the country that seems to belong to your family or husbands. *(Yes. Rachel was born in such a home.)* With wicker chairs in the porch and yard. *(?)*

Very old woman lived there, a relative, like a great grandmother, or great aunt perhaps.

(Rachel's grandmother lived there and brought Rachel up.
(End of session 10:09.
(Rachel Clayton almost "going under" as she watched Jane.
([MD] Data not included with ESP sessions. Cross reference when notes found.)

SESSION 386, ESP CLASS, DECEMBER 7, 1967
APPROXIMATELY 9:50 PM THURSDAY

([MD] Please Note: This session has two versions. The first version is that of Rob Butt's and contains some of his notes. The second portion is Florence McIntyre's version. You will note some differences in Seth's statements. This is Jane's first session without Rob. Both versions are included at Yale.)

([MD]This was an unscheduled session held for Jane's Thursday night ESP class and not planned at all. There were three witnesses present: Andrea Bergere, Rose Cafford and Florence McCullough. Only Florence had witnessed a session before.

([Rob]The unique thing here is that this is Jane's first session at which I was not present. In the light of the materi-

al obtained in the two regular sessions earlier this week, we believe this to be a significant step forward; a mark of Jane's increasing confidence in her psychic ability, and wholehearted acceptance we believe to be necessary.

(Earlier in the day I had heard Jane remark causally, after a little talk between us, that if she felt like it she would let Seth come through during class tonight. When the session began I was at work in my studio at the back of the apartment; yet, through two closed doors, I heard almost at once when the session began. I was working on the index to these sessions at the time, and the place was quiet.

(Since it was Jane's first session without my presence, I thought it would be interesting to record some of it. I opened one of the two doors and made notes; thus the students and Jane were not disturbed on the other side of the remaining closed door. Seth's voice was easily heard.

(I did not get the first few sentences down, but most of the following is verbatim.)

...Those who survive physical death are individuals, as they have always been.

When communication is set up with those within your physical system, then indeed life meets life. You cannot understand nor intellectually grasp pure truth. It therefore must be given in terms that you can understand. In parables.

One part of the self <u>is</u> (underlined) pure truth. The other portions of the personality need translation and interpretation. They do not understand what they are.

You exist in more dimensions than you know, and

your own reality *(voice quite a bit louder and stronger)* transcends your understanding and transcends the limitations of your own intellectual knowledge ... *(pace faster, still fairly loud)* These truths must be understood intuitively... In quiet moments of your existence... *(faster here)* you will know your part in creation ... uniqueness, and your own individuality *(now slower),* for through your own individuality what you call God expresses himself and is known.

The energy that moves through the universe moves the muscles of your hand as you write ... This is what you are after. You have it, but you do not realize the knowledge that you have. The person that you seek is here, but he is with you, and has never parted from you, and even though he continues his existence in another dimension you are not divided nor separated; and you will gain from <u>his</u> added development, for he will telepathically let you understand matters that you did not understand before.

Now we shall let Ruburt take a break, or end the session ... at his discretion ...

(About 9:58. The last few lines above refer to Andrea Bergere's deceased son.)

In any case I greet you most heartily, and I am glad to be here. I have met you but you have not met me. I regret that through the channels of communication my voice does not always sound as genial as I desire—a matter of vocal cords and other mechanisms.

We shall let our friend Ruburt decide whether to end the session.

(10 PM. Seth resumed at about 10:15, briefly, address-

SESSION 386

ing a little reincarnational data to Andrea.)

... A boy. Relatives from Russia. *(Pause.)* Myshurek *(my interpretation)* last name. In... what is now, or what was Warsaw. A trader, a merchant, four children. A French wife.

Earlier in 1242 a Dutch existence. There was a Spanish life in the 13th century and one in what is now the state of California in the very early 1800's. You have been twice a woman, three times a man.

You are developing along certain lines, your interest in the outdoors now reflecting your earlier male existences. We will give you more specific details at a later time. With dates and names.

Now I will indeed leave you, for all practical purposes; though I will be here, I will not speak again this evening.

(10:25.)

SESSION 386, ESP CLASS, DECEMBER 7, 1967

([Florence McIntyre's Version])
(After a serious discussion of the search for truth, life after death, religious backgrounds, etc. at 8:50 PM Jane, without warning, started a Seth session. Attending were Andrea, Rose Cafford and Florence McIntyre. The following notes are as complete as I was able to keep up with Seth.)

I have been listening to you with great interest. I give you all my best wishes and I give you my blessings—

those that I have to give.

You are all here for a reason. You did not come here by chance. Our friend Ruburt is giving me more freedom now, and I shall visit with you more often in our classes. He has not been using his full abilities but he is now learning that he must do so if he is to develop, and if he is to do his best by you, for you are my students, you see, as well as his.

I come here to renew my acquaintance with one of you *(Florence)* and to introduce myself to two of you. We shall become well acquainted. I keep my eye out for your welfare. We shall not have a long session this evening. I shall not give you any outstanding evidential revelation this evening so you may or may not take notes as you desire.

I wanted to make one small point. Those who survive physical death are individuals as they have always been.

When communication is set up with those within your physical system, then indeed, like seeks like. You cannot understand or intellectually grasp pure truth. It therefore must be given in terms that you can understand—in parables.

One part of the self is <u>pure truth</u>. The other portions of the personality need translation and interpretation. They do not understand what they are. You exist in more dimensions than you know and your own reality transcends your own understanding and intellect. They must be understood intuitively. In your quiet moments you will recognize them. You will know your own individuality and your part in creation... *(several words lost here [see Rob's version, p. 12])*.

The energy that moves the universe is the same that moves your hand now. You have it but you do not realize the knowledge that you have. The person you seek is here. He is with you here and has never parted from you. In one sense you are not divided or separated and you will gain from his added development for he will telepathically let you understand matters that you have never understood before.

I regret that due to our method of communication that my voice does not sound as genial. It is due to vocal cords... but my feelings are most friendly.

(After a short break and discussion, Seth again began.)

This will be brief. You *(pointing to Andrea)*, in 1572—Poland, what is now considered Poland, a boy—relatives from Russia. Majurak—last name—ended up in what is now Warsaw—a trader, a merchant—4 children—a French wife—earlier in 1242—a Dutch existence. There was a Spanish life in the 17th century and one in what is now California in the early 1800's. You have been twice a woman and three times a man. You are developing along certain lines. Your interest in the outdoors now reflecting your male existence. We will give you more specific details at a later time with dates and names.

Now I will indeed leave you for all practical purposes though I will be here I will not speak again this PM.

ESP CLASS SESSION, DECEMBER 26, 1967, TUESDAY

(Seth begins his discourse on Harvey McIntyre's dream. Present were Florence and Harvey and their son Daniel, and Rose and Archie Cafford.)

Good evening.

Now we do not have any precognitive dream. Instead, we have the realization of some inner difficulty. In this case, the cellar is the mind. The alligators represent fears, the fears that lie within you; your subconscious. You are afraid your house rests on shifting sands. You fear your fears would devour you and are afraid to go among them. Yet these thoughts that you fear do not represent any real danger. You project fear upon them. They are not harmful. There is a reason the dream comes at this time. There have been others with smaller fears but now larger. You are afraid of losing your footing, you see. The fears have to do largely with experience that may come to pass within a three year period. There are decisions to make, but you are uncertain and disinclined to face yourself fully to reach a decision. This fear is formed into alligators and you disconnect them from your own being. They are perfectly harmless parts of your personality that you have not accepted fully. You fear them because you misinterpret their meaning.

(Seth withdrew, and there was a ten minute break.)

I am here merely to show you I am here. I am not here to prove anything. I am here because you wish me to be here, and I am a kindly old gentleman. I have said this before—I am indeed repeating myself. However, it is no coincidence that you should hear me speak and that we have been drawn together. All of you are aware that there are realities that you cannot see or touch and you are all willing—you are reaching out. If you were not, I would not be here this evening.

You must all remember questions you had when children, and you must never stop asking questions. You must ask yourself where I came from and what my presence has to do with you. I have been where you are. I have been young and old; as I have existed you shall exist. You must develop your abilities now.

I know about all of you. It is because you want to know that I am here. There are many truths you know that you are not aware of. Be still and listen to your inner voice. You are too busy with exterior things.

If there is one thing only I could tell you it would be this. Be still—listen—listen to the voices within you that you have not listened to. You have lived many lives. Some of you will live more lives in this reality. You have gained much wisdom, but you do not listen. I am here, and because I am here I tell you that your own inner self does continue to exist, and as I teach others now, so shall you also be witnesses of the existence of All That Is.

You must face yourself now. You cannot afford to play overlong—to hide yourself in trivia—to become so busy that you cannot hear the truth that shouts within you. I know what the transition is like and I tell you it is pleasant—but your responsibilities will still exist, and you will ask yourself how you have fulfilled them. You must know yourself if you would help others. You must look inward and listen.

ESP CLASS SESSION, DECEMBER 28, 1967 10:15 PM THURSDAY

(Session addressed to Andrea Bergere, whose adopted son died by drowning last summer.)

In a previous life he was your son by blood. He died in that life in an accident. He came back to tell you there was no death—you would not listen, hear or believe. This time he came back and was a son to you. You knew him again under circumstances highly similar. This time you are listening. He came to tell you there was no death. You have been led here—you are to develop your abilities. This was his last reincarnation. He chose to stay here to tell you. You had too little faith in him. That you thought...

You have been given a privilege and gift. He came back under his own free will to teach you.

Without this knowledge you could not progress in the way you are now. He is teaching you. (Teach you love—he would not die.)

Without this knowledge you would not progress. Consciousness of this boy is indeed alive. Work in this life is completed, reincarnation cycle completed.

SESSION 12/28/1967

Had the boy continued, there would have been complications. Marriage and children for his own nature. Main purpose was with you for you had been mother. Death was instantaneous. There was some recognition on your part. The boy knew this and understood it.

There was in past life connection with your brother. He was also connected with you and the boy. The brother in this life was the blood father as you were blood mother. Boy's first love and purpose involved you.

He knew only he could teach you this lesson, and no one else whose death would affect you so strongly.

In past he also died by water. Subconsciously you knew this. There was a girl in that past life. He also knew her in this life. There was an afternoon in this life between 4 and 5 years old, and this child visited with her parents. She also will die young or has already died but will not reach adulthood. At the time curly brown hair. She was his wife in the past life, when he died at 32. This involved a shipwreck. Now the manner of death is no coincidence, it is chosen. Some of the boy's friends and acquaintances and neighbors died in this same manner. They were the crew in a ship that sank off coast of Spain. They were not frightened of water. They trusted water. If it led on occasion to death, it also led to adventure. Death by water in those days was an honor, death by land a disgrace. They considered water "Mother of all Earth." He did. He would not want to die by land.

He chose to leave when he did, when you would miss him most and question most. For the question would lead you to find answers. He played the harmonica as a sailor. Love of music at first—the result of long days at sea.

I have no particular love for water so I can't explain its meaning for him. To him it meant release and freedom. This time he is truly free for he feels you understand. It is important you understand what lies behind his messages and concern!

ESP CLASS SESSION, FEBRUARY 8, 1968
9:25 PM THURSDAY

(This session witnessed by: Coral Bishop, Susie Nolan, Lillian Nelson, Janet Clifton and Bonnie Anderson. Notes by Rob.

(Jane's voice was somewhat stronger and more forceful than usual, and quite serious.)

Now, good evening. I wish you all a fond good evening.

("Good evening Seth.")

I have said this before and I will indeed say it many times again: those of you who come here, come here for a reason.

You are at a particular point in your existence and it is a time for you to learn and to develop. You are at a point where you are ready to look into yourselves, and to take the next steps that must indeed be taken.

You are ready to expand your own consciousness.

SESSION 2/8/1968

You are ready to learn about your past lives and to prepare for your future ones. Do not be frightened of me. On occasion I can be a very humorous and kindly gentleman. This evening however I am concerned with your education, and when I am concerned with your education I am apt to be rather dry.

All of you were meant to come here and your lives have already been changed. They have been changed in beneficial ways—you have already begun to question your existence. Before you came here you wondered. You are ready now to embark upon the inner roads of your own existence.

All of those now in this room are coming close to their last reincarnations, and when these are done you must know yourselves thoroughly. It has been meant that help be given to you. It is also meant that you use your own abilities. Therefore, for most of you there are two or three existences in the physical plane still left for you. If you do not understand yourselves there will be more.

Subconsciously you all know this, and so you come here; and because you have come here do I speak to you.

(Now Jane, as Seth, pointed to Bonnie.) One I have known vaguely in my own past. However, you would not recognize me now, though I do indeed remember you. Now, you would not know yourself, for you were a small boy of three to four years old when I knew you, and I did not know you well. This was in Denmark, and your father was a baker. You had indeed a very short life, dying at nine or ten, of diphtheria. You see, you are older than you

knew you were.

(Smile. Many times before Seth has told us he lived a life in Denmark in the sixteenth century.)

For some time you have all been searching, and I hope to show you how to ask the proper questions; for in the questions you will find the answers, and in the answers you shall be yourselves; and knowing yourselves fulfill your purpose and expand the limitations of your own consciousness until you can search out the past and the present and see yourselves as you are, and know that you are more than you think you are, and fulfill those abilities which you have partially developed in past lives.

Within you there is indeed innate knowledge of all the selves that you have been, and all the selves that you shall be, and this knowledge sustains you even when you do not know consciously that it exists.

I have been biding my time, seeking for the most auspicious moment in which to speak to you, and to announce my presence—for I am here in these classes, as indeed Ruburt knows that I am.

You may now take a break and we shall continue the session or end it, as always at your convenience. And you may tell Ruburt for me, Joseph *(smile)*, that I thank him ...

([Rob:] "For what?")

... that he has welcomed me. Tell him that I shall see to it that he learns what he wants to know.

(9:52. Jane came out of trance. The last lines above referred to a discussion Jane and I had earlier in the day.

(Bonnie Anderson now told us that for many years she has had a fear of diphtheria, strange as it seems. At break Lillian commented that she thought Jane's delivery as Seth sounded Germanic. She also said that when speaking as Seth, Jane tended to use the same gestures and facial wrinkles shown in the portrait I have painted of Seth.

(At break reincarnation was naturally discussed, with Lillian voicing some doubts on this score. Session resumed at 10: 05. Seth pointed at Lillian.)

Now, we shall shortly end our session.

However, you will reincarnate whether or not you believe that you will. It is much easier if your theories fit reality, but if they do not, then you do not change reality one iota. Give us a moment here.

1832 ... Near a place now called Bangor, Maine. You spent 41 years there, a slim man. I will give these impressions as they come. Richita *(or Wichita?—my phonetic interpretation.)*. An Indian name... a war that is not Indian against white man, but Indian and white man against Indian and white man. Not nationality but trade. This occurring somewhat further west but in the same general area, involving Indians down from Canada and an 1852 or 1856 resolution of this battle.

He then had two children. One child now the present husband, and one a very distant relative.

([Rob:] "What was his name?")

Son-of-the-Northern Willows. In your language R, A, K, E, S *(spelled);* either Andrus or Andrew as the first name and a French background here also. Buried, however, near Lake Champlain, to the northwest in an old burial ground.

(Jane, as Seth, again pointed to Lillian.) His daughter then marrying a man called Lines, a merchant. Difficulties in the left leg from an old wound. Also difficulties with the right ear and teeth. An overreliance upon emotionalism then, and a headstrong attitude, little given to reason. This time an effort being made to right those characteristics.

A half-sister at that time. Miranda Charbeau, from a French side of the family, who married into an English branch, into the Franklin Bacon family of Boston.

Now *(in a quieter voice) I* am here this evening merely to tell you that I am here. I am not here to do wonders. I am here to tell you that I have survived physical death, and that you have survived physical death time and time again. Quite simply, this is my message to you this evening, and I bid you a fond good evening...

And I am aware of many things that you think and do not say. Do not be afraid of old age, you who are so young, for you have been old many times before. And you are young now, and you learned from each lifetime, as indeed, you shall learn from this lifetime. *(Smile).*

("Goodnight Seth. "

(10:20. As I suspected, the .session was not yet over. During break Lillian told us that she had lived in Bangor as a preschool child, and had been very attached to Maine; so much so that when she left there to move to New York State, she at first refused to say she lived in NYS. Lillian also told

us that she had many relatives in Boston, Mass.)

(Resume at 10:30.)

The name begins with an O.

(Here Seth refers to a discussion during break, concerning some of the previous data; I cannot now pinpoint what was questioned. Jane thinks the O may refer to the name Rakes. One of the witnesses may remember and a space is left below for any notes.)

Now give me a moment, Joseph.

(Seth pointed to Janet Clifton.) Here... Mesopotamia, before it was known by that name. *(Pause.)* And here we do find abilities shown, ignored and misused through a succession of lives. A rather classic example of the progress followed by many psychically-endowed, but in poor control of their personalities and abilities.

China and Egypt, lives in various religious capacities, however, without the necessary sense of responsibility. Unfortunately taking advantage instead of the fortunes made available to those in ruling classes throughout the ages. For this reason the abilities have not as yet come to fruition. Only in this existence is there finally some understanding, and a growing sense of responsibility. The personality in the past used psychic abilities for the wrong purposes. Therefore, they did not fully develop and the personality was at a standstill.

There was a death by fire on two occasions. *(Pause.)* There has been a dabbling in occult matters and some chicanery. The personality relying largely upon its own resources. 1524... Ireland... 1721, a small town 25 meters from Charterous. *(Pause.)* The nearest approximation here: C, H, A, R... *(spelling unfinished)*, Charteris. *(Pause. My phonetic interpretation.)*

Manupelt. *(Again my phonetic interpretation. Jane as Seth repeated the word.)*

([Rob:] "Can you spell that?")

M, A, N, A, U, P, *(pause)* A, U, L, T the last name. A curia. *(Pause)* Some connection here with the first historical personality whom we have run across: a very far distant connection to Joan of Arc, on the mystic's father's side, twice removed. And that name, approximately as given, in some records.

([Rob:] "Where would the records be?")

An old cathedral. In... of... the name that I have given you. The family name, the town and the cathedral name are the same.

Now my dear friend, Joseph, I have Ruburt in a good state. Do you have any questions for me that can be answered here now?

([Rob:] "How is it possible for you to know this information?")

(Smile.) We have had our sessions for how long now... and you ask me this?

([Rob:] "I just wanted you to explain it to the people present.")

Very well. Your idea of time is false. Time as you experience it is an illusion caused by your own physical senses. Your physical senses force you to perceive action in certain terms, but this is not the nature of action.

You must perceive what you do of reality through your physical senses, but your physical senses distort reality. They present reality to you in their own way. The physical senses can only perceive reality a little bit at a time, and so it seems to you that one moment exists, and is gone forever, and the next moment comes, and like the one before it disappears. But everything in the universe exists at one time, simultaneously, and the first words ever spoken still ring throughout the universe; and in your terms, the last words ever spoken have been said time and time again, for there is no ending and no beginning. It is only your perception that is limited.

Reality is not limited. There is no past, present and future. These only appear to those who exist within three-dimensional reality. Since I am no longer within it, I can perceive what you do not see. But there is a part of you that is not imprisoned within three-dimensional reality, and that part of you knows that there is no time, that there is only an eternal now; and that part of you that knows is the whole self, the inner personality that knows all of your lives.

When I tell you that you have lived for example in 1936, I say this because it makes sense to you now; but you live all of your reincarnations at once. Only you are not aware, and you cannot understand within the framework of three-dimensional reality.

Pretend that you have seven dreams at once and you the dreamer know that you are dreaming. Within each dream 100 earthly years may pass —but to you the dreamer no time has passed, and there is no time to pass, for you are free of the dimension in which time exists. The time you seem to spend within the dream, within each life, is only an illusion, and to the inner self no moment has passed, and to the inner self there is no time.

([Rob:] "Thanks Seth. "

(End at 10:55. Jane, as Seth, had delivered the last material, on time, rapidly and in an impassioned manner.

(Janet Clifton now told us that she has always had a fear of fire. Also, Joan of Arc has figured rather prominently in her life; in school for instance she was called Joan of Arc, witch, etc.)

ESP CLASS SESSION, FEBRUARY 20, 1968 TUESDAY

Now, I have been here listening. We are having some difficulties with our friend's voice and as you see he has worn a skirt rather than slacks which somehow hamper activities.

Now we are beginning to study my material. Now I shall be close by for the material is the best that I can give you. There are hints there of basic truths. Any speech within your system and expression must be tinged and must be somewhat distorted in order to make sense to you.

Basic reality has no need for words. Words are but symbols, but without symbols you cannot intellectually understand what I have to say to you, and so I must use them. There are questions that you would ask me, and I shall answer them in time and as the opportunity presents itself.

Your idea of reality will indeed begin to change and you must learn to manipulate within the new system as you learn of it for the old rules will no longer apply. You will not be able to get along in the old way for learning entails new responsibilities and so you must stretch and grow. My material in many ways will not make things easier for you. You will demand more of yourselves. You will give more. You will insist that you learn to use your own abilities. I will not give you answers. I will show you the questions, and I will attempt to lead you to answers. Your own intuitions will guide you, and they shall awaken as you study.

I shall be watching your progress. Though I have no gold stars to give you, you may leave Ruburt an apple. I anticipate a most enjoyable time and indeed if you have questions then you can receive the answers from the horse's mouth.

Now, your toy does not do you justice but we shall put up with it.

You are in your apprenticeship period, and soon we shall see how you can develop and what you can produce. There are joys and advantages that will come as a result of your studies. They will come if you allow yourselves to open up to your inner selves. They will come as you learn to use your own inner senses, and the material will explain what these inner senses are and how you can use them.

We are now embarking upon a new point in your classes and if my friend Ruburt will allow me you shall have at times another teacher for I shall step in now and then to provide my own demonstrations. It goes without saying that certain conditions must be indeed be met. Circumstances must be beneficial. Any words of mine will always be spoken to quicken your own education for as I have said often, I am an educator and that is my main purpose and my purpose in this class. If any demonstrations occur they will occur only when the moment is right, and they will happen as a side issue to demonstrate certain points which should be made. I will try to give you information that I know you want to have, but at times I will also give you information that you may not wish to have.

You and you alone are responsible for your own development. No one can develop your own abilities but you. I am here and I have been here often in your classes.

It is because you have yourselves reached a certain point in your own development that I speak to you tonight, and when I do so I am between systems. I am neither here nor there, you see. I am using Ruburt's nervous system, for example, but I am not Ruburt. I come to you from a long way and yet the distance is not in terms of space. I am separated from you in a way that has nothing to do with space. May I say that I do indeed enjoy this situation, now being indeed the only gentleman present. I am endeavoring, you see, to let more of my personality show itself this evening [so] that you can know me by my characteristics as well as my words. If you do not like the one you may prefer the other.

But when I speak to you of death, know that I myself have died and been reborn many times before. Yet I speak to you and I speak in a lively manner, for one dead. Therefore, when you are tempted to think of it as an end of all, then remember that you know a rather lively spirit and when you hear my voice speaking through Ruburt this evening then remember how hoarse it was before I began to speak, and know indeed that were I not such a gentleman, I could add considerably to its volume. The hour is late however and Ruburt would not thank me for my troubles. He would worry about the neighbors.

Now when circumstances are good we had better take advantage of them. I shall not keep you long. I could indeed go on, myself, like this for hours but I shall take into consideration your human failings and I know you need such things as sleep. I am indeed coming through very well this evening, very well, however, and if I may say so I am in somewhat of a frisky mood. However, and this is to show you that your so-called spirits are not always long-faced and somber. I am at times, I admit, mischievous. You must realize that basic reality is joyful and that the way of life upon which I hope you shall embark is joyful, and if my actions and communication can show you this then I have done well indeed. Now, it will not particularly serve any great or awesome purpose for me to thus appear in this guise nor to raise my voice in a way quite impossible for this rather puny young woman, and yet because the circumstances are so auspicious I am so tempted.

This does not mean that the demonstration serves no purpose, for all of my demonstrations serve a purpose and this one is to show that there is indeed a vitality that lives beyond the grave and that there is joy, and the personality continues to exist for this most willing and friendly associative man can permit me to speak in the most fearless and carefree tones. For this is hardly the end and I am here to tell you it is quite possible for me to continue on such a demonstration until your very eardrums will plead to me for mercy. However, I shall not do so.

This scribbling goes slowly. Now, I am aware that I shall have some small difficulties with my friend but he, Ruburt, understands. When circumstances are at their best then he allows me to come through clearly, but he is concerned over issues that are only of surface importance as far as the volume of the voice is concerned, and he is only now learning control. I will end our session again because I understand that your hour is late. Your hour has little to do with me however and I merely defer to your wishes.

I offer my heartiest regards and I do indeed offer those blessings which are mine to give. On some occasions I may come through with greater or lesser effectiveness. Now I am here in a fairly undistorted form and you will recognize me and remember me when I come here again, and I will know you. I will not forget you for now

I feel I know you all very well indeed.

(*In a whisper.*) Now *[we]* shall annoy no one. Shall I simply sit here and radiate or shall I speak? I do not like to offend Ruburt and such indeed is not my intention. I am here this evening to show you that death does not automatically change you into a somber long-faced ghost. I am here to show you that I am myself, and you shall be yourselves.

One small note here *(to Rachel). You* have nothing to worry about along the terms of which you spoke earlier this evening. It was your inner fear that caused the dream. You were however in contact with your grandmother. I wanted to speak to you in less remote terms than usual. I wanted to convey to you the fact that the personality is composed of indestructible elements and that these elements are never destroyed. I wanted you to feel the impact of my personality as you would feel the impact of any living personality. I wanted, in other words, to speak to you as a person. I am going to leave you now.

ESP CLASS SESSION, FEBRUARY 29, 1968
10 PM THURSDAY

(*Seth session, spontaneous, during class. From notes taken by Lillian and Janet during class.*)

I will come through in this class when circumstances permit. Some of you objected when I said *(in the only other session held for this class)* that you were meant to come here. You felt, perhaps, pushed. The fact is that you were at the point where you were seeking answers to questions, and you were seeking new questions. You were led by your inner selves to any place where these questions might be answered. My material will indeed change your lives.

You hope, you dream, that your lives will be creative... *(phrase left out)* and that is why you are here. Others are not here. You are here because you want to learn, and understand the various dimensions of your own reality. You sense something of which you have not been told. I will be here again whether or not I speak to you. I am here this evening to tell you that when conditions are to our satisfaction, I will speak to you and answer your questions.

There are realities and dimensions which you sense, and you are correct. They are outside the recognized systems of knowledge. The questions you ask are not considered legitimate within the recognized schools of knowledge. My very *[presence?]* must make you think. Within the material you will find a framework, and this framework will allow you to understand what reality is. It will allow you to wake up and see the camouflage that you call physical reality.

I should not be here, according to what you have been taught. According to what you have been taught, I do not exist, and yet I can assure you that I do exist. What happens in this room should not happen, according to what you have been taught, and yet it happens. It is enough to open up your own inner senses, to show you that more exists than what you have been told.

Do you think that when you grow old you will become shriveled and come to nothing? Such is far from the case. Indeed, then as a "nothing," I speak very loudly. When circumstances permit I shall make myself rather better known in this room... There are certain rules that my friend Ruburt places upon me, one that I hold my voice under control, and so I will endeavor to do so.

I have said that vitality in the personality *is* vitality in the personality. Because I have left your planet doesn't mean that I must be somber and speak in somber tones. Existence... does not presuppose sobriety. Existence is joyful, and vitality rings throughout the universe, and speaks out indeed with such a voice as mine. To be blessed is not to go about with a long face.

You can use your intellect and your emotions. One need not block out the others. The ideas in my material will open up your eyes, your inner eyes. You will begin to look at your universe as you have never looked at it before. The camouflage world is beautiful, but more exists that you do not see. Look where you see nothing with your physical eyes, and you shall find *(much?)* that will amaze you. Listen where you hear nothing, and you will hear much that will amaze you. Now my friend Ruburt may take a break or end the session as he prefers. I myself am delighted to speak to you. I have been here since you entered the room and I shall be here until you leave it. You know more than you realize, and your own inner knowledge will always propel you to find the answers that you seek... On some occasion I will speak in a less weighty manner. I am [restrained] by the vehicle through which I speak. I do indeed give you the blessings that are mine to give.

(Break 10:17. Session began at 10 PM.
(Resume at 10:27.)

Now according to what you have been taught, my friend Ruburt should be mad *(crazy)* but he is not. According to what you have been told, you are created of physical matter and you cannot escape it, and this is not so. According to what you have been taught, you must disintegrate as you grow old and this is not so. The physical matter of which you are seemingly composed will disintegrate *(in physical death)* but you will not disintegrate.

Though you cannot find me, you know that I am here. Though your own parents seem to disappear before your eyes and vanish into eternity forever, so it seems that all that you are will also disappear. I can assure you that your parents will live. I can assure you that death is another beginning, that when you are dead, you are not silenced. For is this silence? Is this presence that you sense here now within this room, death? I am more alive than many who walk the face of your planet now. More alive than some of your professors and friends, for aliveness is dependent upon the state of your consciousness, dependent upon your awareness, your ability to perceive and to feel.

I am here to tell you that your joy [is] not dependent upon your youth, for I am hardly young. I am here to tell you that your joy is not dependent upon your physical body, for I have none. I am here to tell you that your joy is not dependent upon your nervous system or physical form, since I have none. I have what I have always had, the identity that is mine. It is never diminished. It grows and develops.

You are what you are, and you shall be more. Don't be afraid of change, for you are change, and you change as you sit before me. All action consists of change, for otherwise there would be a static universe, and indeed death would then be the end. As Seth you know me as an old man, but I have been a young woman. Change joyfully.

(This is difficult to explain. Here we took a break. Lillian began to read the notes she had taken and Seth corrected them as she read, so that there was a constant give and take going on.)

I am here to tell you that what you are is not even dependent upon what you feel or touch... You cannot touch me and yet you know I am here in the room...

What I am is also what you are... I am individualized consciousness and so are you.

Do not be afraid but change with the seasons, for you are more than the seasons and you form the seasons, as they are the reflections of your psychic climate. *(This was a phrase left out earlier. Seth spoke so quickly it was difficult to take notes.)* I had better leave you, for you are indeed mad scribblers. We need a recorder for if I speak naturally, you cannot take it down.

I have come for one purpose, so that you could sense my vitality and sensing this, know that I speak to you from dimensions beyond those with which you are acquainted. The grave is not the end, for so noisy a one never spoke with the lips of death.

I am joyful though there is no physical heart that I have claim to. And I am in this room, though there is no object within which you can place me. And you are not within any object. You are as disembodied as I. You have a vehicle to use, a body that you call your own, and this is all. I borrow Ruburt's, with his consent, but what I am is not dependent upon atoms or molecules, and what you are is not dependent upon physical matter. Your own consciousness is part of each season. You are not limited by the bones of your skull.

You have lived before and you are living now and you will live again. And when you are done with physical existence you will still live.

I can enjoy your earthly days when I so choose, and stroll disembodied down your spring streets, and look through Ruburt's eyes at the winter nights. And when you learn what you must learn, you will be able to look back to the pasts that you have known, and ahead to the days that you will know, for there is no end because there was no beginning. You always have been and you always will be. This is the meaning of existence and joy. The God that is, is within you, for you are a part of All That Is.

And through my voice you hear a very small echo of All That Is.

(Voice very loud and powerful here. Janet said though she knew it was corning from me, Jane, still it seemed to come from all around the room.)

There are realities and systems within this room that you do not *(consciously)* perceive, but your inner senses perceive them.

I come to you as though I appeared through a hole in space and time. There are walks *[warps?]* in space and time through which you can travel—and in dreams you have been where I am. You are dreaming. You have yet to awaken. The inner senses will allow you to awaken, and to see the awakening reality behind your dream.

My friend Ruburt may take a break or end the session as he prefers. You may think of me as an old man and yet my joy circles this room as a bluebird might fly from corner to corner. And my essence, like air, fills the room as your essence, like air, fills the room.

(Break 11:13 PM.

(First phrases after resumption lost. Seth came back suddenly.)

You have done very well and I commend you *(to Lillian)*. I have been cautioned by my friend, and so I shall not keep you longer. I have tried to tell you this evening of realities with which you are deeply involved, whether or not you realize it.

I want you to feel your own vitality. Sit quietly for some moments in a room alone and feel your own identity grow and reach out. Feel it travel through the universe and know that it is not dependent upon your physical image. For you form your own physical universe—it does not form you.

You are in a dream. The dreamer says that physical reality forms you. In reality you project your psychic energy outward unto the physical universe. Therefore, to change your world you change that which you project.

ESP CLASS SESSION, MARCH 12, 1968 TUESDAY

Now I am coming to you briefly for a very simple reason—to let you know you are indeed welcome here and that you do not bother our friend Ruburt. He is less easily bothered of late in any case. We have not had a session while you have been here, and I did not want you to think that I had anything against you, you know. I will not interfere, for I know you have some business with your table to attend to. I simply wanted you to know that I was here, as I said I would be.

Give me a moment please...

Now, I will consider the situation in which you are involved *(pointing to Florence),* and we shall discuss it at a session as soon as possible. There is indeed a complication arising in part from past-life connections, but also in the early background of the woman involved. The problem must be worked out by her, and she must find the support within herself, you see. She is not considering others but only herself, but from the torment within herself she is projecting the situation. There is advice that will help her and I will go into the situation more thoroughly in a regular session. I will also go into another matter of which you have spoken, and it was I indeed who gave Ruburt the insight today into a certain aspect of that problem.

Now I will let you get on with your class, and if I do not come through like the voice of spring you must forgive me. I enjoy being here. I quite intend to attend your classes. I shall see what a good teacher your Ruburt is, and I shall correct him if he makes errors.

I am in the position of teaching Ruburt and Joseph, and their responsibility is to teach others. They could accept this situation or not. The choice was up to them. Their own development however would not be as complete had they chosen to ignore the responsibility. They know me and they have known me well in past lives, you see, so I was not the stranger to them that they thought I was. This is their last reincarnation, and I tell you it is much easier to solve your problems now than to solve them later, and they are solving theirs now. And in solving theirs, they are helping others also.

Ruburt has always had a difficulty—if he will forgive me—in integrating the various abilities that are his. He was either so intellectual that you could not understand him when he spoke or so intuitive that you could not understand him when he spoke. The duty he imposed upon himself this time was to integrate these two strong aspects of himself, and he has had his difficulties in doing so. We have known each other many times, Ruburt and

Joseph and I.

Now, though I joke with you because I must speak now through a woman, as I have told you, I have been a woman, and so the strangeness is not as strong as I sometimes pretend.

Your own entity knows your strong points and your weak points, and it gives you life situations and it hopes that you will solve these problems. No one makes you solve these problems. You can accept them or run away from them. No one tells you that you must develop. Nevertheless, the desire to develop is within you. You will find your own way. I have been where you are. I am now within the space that you inhabit in this room. You will one day be where I am, and you will have learned many things. I can point the way to you but you must follow that way on your own.

Now, whenever you are truly joyful, you are on the right track. No god ever meant or intended that you suffer. God is a joyful being. To the extent that you do not realize that you exist in Him are you sorrowful. To the extent that you do <u>not</u> develop your abilities and project them into physical realities are you sorrowful. To the extent that you do <u>not</u> live up to your potential are you sorrowful. It is indeed true that you find yourself by losing yourself. You are indeed a part of All That Is. When you attempt to concentrate on the tiny I that you imagine yourself, then indeed you do not know where you are and you cannot find yourself.

Now, you see what you have done to my intentions.

I came here merely to give greetings to our new friend here and I find myself immediately involved in philosophical discussion. But while I find it fun to speak to you, because I am a teacher, you see, I cannot leave it at that. I must always make a point and each time I come here, though my words are meaningless, do I make a point. My very presence in this room makes a point though the words were gibberish and I can assure you that whatever else they may be, my words will not be gibberish!

Out of the goodness of my invisible heart, I will let our friend Ruburt rest, but be assured that I am not some general mass of invisible protoplasm, you see. I am myself and I shall always be myself and I am aware of you as you are and there can indeed be a give and take between us. For again, I have been where you are, and where I am, dear friends, so shall you one day be!!

(Seth withdrew and there was a class break.)

Now there is no place in those terms. In the first place there is no such thing as a place—no heaven in terms of a location. You form your ideas of space. Existence forms its own reality. Your physical senses form your idea of space. This same so called space within this room also contains me and others like me. Space is your illusion. With your physical senses you only recognize a small portion of reality. That which you recognize, you call physical. But more exists within what you call the space of this room, and you do not perceive it.

Consciousness takes up no space in your terms. It

forms what space is. When consciousness needs space in which to operate, it creates space. When it is resting it does not need space and it does not create it in these terms. It becomes concentrated energy falling back in upon itself in sleep and rest. Knowledge within your brain does not take up physical space within your brain. Dreams help form your personality, but they do not take up physical space. Your personality does not take up physical space. What you are exists independently of both space and time. When you are resting between reincarnations, you rest in a dimension in terms of space and time. You come back into space and time if you desire to reincarnate. Where I am, space and time as you define it, do not exist. I can take advantage of them to some degree to speak to you, but to me they are transparent and they do not basically exist.

Now, Ruburt's eyes work much better when I am in control of them. I see each of you now with Ruburt's eyes closed as you have been in past reincarnations and as you will be. And with Ruburt's eyes closed there is some difficulty for I must focus psychically in order to find you as you think you are now, for I see all of you. I see all of what you are. But it is difficult for me, with Ruburt's eyes closed, for me to see you as you imagine yourself to be at this particular point in space and time. With Ruburt's eyes open, I can see you as he sees you as a particular personality in this particular space and time and then, you see, I can place you within your own development.

Now briefly, we will continue while Ruburt learns

how to manipulate his controls. In dreams you communicate with your own past lives. In dreams you often know who you have been. In dreams you often realize what you have learned. In dreams you restate your challenges and problems. In waking reality, subconsciously you manipulate atoms and molecules so that they result in physical images that appear to you as permanent. They are not permanent. The atoms and molecules as you know, constantly change. But they retain enough semblance of permanency so that you can rely upon their position in space, their size and weight and their depth and physical dimension. You can agree as to their placement in space.

Now in dreams you also form your environment. The dream locations that you visit you form in precisely the same manner as atoms and molecules, but they are of briefer duration, for you do not focus your energy upon them for the same amount of physical time. These locations and these dreams appear private to you. You feel that you do not share them with any other. The fact is that you <u>do</u> to a certain extent share them and telepathically, dreams can be dreamed by more than one person.

You form whatever reality that you know. You have always done this. The heaven and hell that you think of, this is your own experience, the consequences of your actions. There is in some distant, ultimate time, a returning to that from which you have come. But when you return to that from which you have come, when you return to what you think of as God, by then new creativity will have already begun, consciousness will evolve in new ways and there will be new challenges.

There is no end. This does not mean that there is no peace, for peace is within you now. If you would but realize it, it is within you. It is closer to you than breath. It is closer to you than your own pulse. It is as close to you as air.

You are co-creators. What you call God is the sum of all consciousness and yet the whole is more than the sum of its parts. God is more than the sum of all personalities, and yet all personalities is what He is. There is constant creation, but peace is to be found in creation. There is a force within you that allows you to breathe. There is a force within you that knew how to grow you from a fetus to a grown adult. This force is part of the innate knowledge within all consciousness and it is a part of the God within you.

The responsibility for your life and your world is indeed yours. It has not been forced upon you by some outside agency. You form your own dreams and you form your own physical reality. I told Ruburt today that God has given you the greatest of all gifts and the most awesome. He has given you what you want. The world is what you want as individuals and as races. The world is what you are. You look at the state of the world and you find the physical materialization of the inner selves which have formed it. You look at nature and you find the joy that is within you that you have also formed outward. You look at the good and it is a reflection of the good that is within you, within each individual person, multiplied outward millions of times for each individual within the planet. And there is no man that hates but that hatred is reflected outward and made physical. And there is no man that loves but that that love is not reflected outward and made physical.

(Seth withdrew and during a discussion, Theodore remarked to Jane, "Must be Seth, your husband and you were old drinking companions in a previous incarnation.")

We were, indeed. Our slight friend Ruburt here was indeed upon occasion, a rather lecherous old fellow, and I was a saintly type. I was, forgive me, his mother. Now I am attempting to set up here with you a personal contact, not for myself but for you.

I want you to realize that you as you understand yourselves to be, your individuality, is not changed by this. I have had this same personality with some minor changes throughout the ages, and you are stuck with yours as I am stuck with mine. All the abilities that I have now I have always had. And you have abilities that you are not using, you see, and the sooner you learn to use them the better it will be for you. I want you to realize that while I no longer inhabit your physical system, the human personality that is mine and thus has filled many physical forms, still exists. I am still learning. I still have work to do and you will still have work to do. You will set challenges for yourselves.

There is a short time between lives when you rest and when you take stock of what you have learned and where you are. But true peace is within you now. And if you do not realize it, it is not because peace does not exist. It is because you have closed yourselves off from peace, and joy springs out of peace. Joy cannot come from unease and dissatisfaction. You will not find peace after this unless you know peace within yourselves now. The kingdom of peace is not on some planet, not four blocks down and three blocks across, not a million light years away and miraculously will you find it. The kingdom of peace is within each of you now and if you realize this, then indeed you dwell in peace and from peace comes your security and confidence and joy.

Now, Ruburt and I banter, we banter back and forth and I am a rare one and he is a rare one, but all of this is based on spiritual understanding and on peace, and joy do you have. You may cough. Have a good one. Do you have any idea of the energy it takes for me to speak to you in terms like this or the degree of manipulation which Ruburt needs and I need? For indeed I have no wish to burst his lungs apart. Yet I tell you that this bit of energy is minute and nothing in comparison to the energy that is within each of you now and that you are not using. The energy that you are not using and the abilities that are yours.

Now, my friend Ruburt has sent me certain signals—they say the voice is too loud, the neighbors will complain. He is most possibly correct. I will therefore leave you, but I remember you, and you shall remember my words. I have, after all, not come here for nothing.

MAY 22, 1968 [WEDNESDAY—NOTES BY JANE ROBERTS] NOTES ON CLASS EVENTS OF MAY 21, 1968

During class, with the lights on, Rose Cafford suddenly said that she saw my aura. She has been able to see auras for years on some occasions, so has Rachel Clayton, I think. Vera and Theodore were then able to see it; and Sally, everyone but Florence, I believe. Without telling them what I was trying to do, I concentrated on making my aura brighter, saying to myself, fire bright. Almost immediately Rose, Sally and Rachel said that the aura was suddenly extremely bright; did this several times. (I had never seen an aura.) It also changed color. They said that, alone, it was white and quite wide and easily noticeable.

I was in the rocker; all lights on. Then various others sat in the rocker. I personally then was able to see auras on Rachel, Theodore and Sally. Position of onlookers seemed to make a difference. It made no difference where persons were sitting though, when we were looking at <u>their</u> auras. (They didn't have to be in rocker, for example.)

I had a feeling we might be able to try something. We turned most of the lights off; at one point all were off though there was some light from the streets. The auras, oddly enough, were more easily seen by us in the light.

Then, with shades down and a candle in another part of the room we sat at big green table. I said, "If there's anyone here, give us a sign," etc.; mentioned my inexperience with physical phenomena and said that ectoplasm would be great if possible. Now three or four of us definitely noticed a fog or mist in part of living room away from table, deeper in the interior of the room. Some of us had been smoking earlier, not now. Would the smoke show up more in the dark? None was noticeable with lights on earlier, and the mist seemed to move, from one side of the coffee table to the other. Sally said that sometimes she could see a painting on the far wall and at other times the mist obscured it.

Then we sat around coffee table with lights on, and lighted candle down to the end of the table. Aloud I asked for the candlelight to change, for the flame to rise. Instead, I felt a strange feeling of extension above my head and before I could comment on it, Rose and someone else —Sally?—called out that my aura had changed color and was now purple. Several more times this happened, aura changes taking place while I subjectively experienced this extension—the same feeling I have in the new sessions with Rob. Definitely not imagination, anyhow; quite definite; I'd say, physical, though the "physical" feeling is where no physical part of me is. No suggestions were given as to aura here, though finally I did tell them when I had the feeling and ask if there was an aura change. This the most vivid experience to me of the night.

The following is most vivid to the students and happened right after the above. I said I'd try something, without giving any indication of what I would try. Though earlier, as mentioned, I did mention ectoplasm, perhaps several times. I concentrated on doing something to my arms, or having someone else do it. Mentally asked for help, think I had ectoplasmic arm in mind. Instead felt as if fingers of left hand were extending.

Sally and Rose said that something was happening to my left hand, which was held out; arm resting on chair rest. (Don't know if I felt the subjective feeling before or after their comments, but no suggestions as to hand was given by me, and I asked no questions, sitting with eyes closed, concentrating, rather in good trance, but aware of their comments. Sally asked me a direct question, and I couldn't answer.) Here everyone in the room with the exception of Theodore who was in a poor position, reported the following:

Watching the hand in transition, changes apparent as they happened, joints and knuckles becoming very thick and large, flesh seeming to disappear so that hand became thinner otherwise, hand taking on the look of a very old woman's, exceedingly bony, with the large, they said, exceptionally large, joints obvious; Rose frightened; Sally said the hand looked so stiff that it was here she asked me if I could bend the fingers, it was here I couldn't answer her but did try to bend the hand; and at this point decided to give myself suggestions to come out of trance and for hand to return to normal. Afterwards, a comparison of hand as it was normally, with what they saw. I wondered if just the light? suggestion? But no suggestion had been given. My own hands are bony—but no, Rose said that my hand now was the normal hand of a young woman and it definitely had been an old woman's hand; a very old woman's hand. Everyone agreed on this—even Florence—but Theodore. He thought that perhaps my hand had gone to sleep—it hadn't—don't know how much time this took, perhaps ten minutes all in all, with hand manifestation taking up... three to five minutes?

Present were Florence, Rose, Rachel, Sally, Theodore, Vera. I believe three of them also mentioned a finger extension, that is, my fingers seemed to get longer and bonier; this was my subjective definite feeling; as definite as the extension sensation earlier over the head. (Theodore saw something with hand, but didn't know what.)

During this same time that hand manifestation was going on, and seen by all but Theodore clearly, other manifestations were reported by Vera, and by her alone. She sat kitty corner from me, diagonally in a clear line. She said that she definitely saw something green, like a green line, going up and down in front of me; also another color, I forget; and that this continued while the hand bit did. Someplace in here, they also reported that part of the astral form was present; or at least the aura was visible down around the shoulders and waist.

Earlier—I'd forgotten—telling them anything except that I was going to try something—I concentrated on trying to form features out from my face. I said mentally, "Out, out, out," trying to project my energy outward in a particular direction. Here Theodore said that he thought [he] saw a filmy whitish something move out from me in the same direction. In here also I concentrated on a ectoplastic arm without telling anyone and Theodore again reported without any suggestion from me that he thought he noticed a change in the same arm, and once thought it was about to rise. I had mentioned nothing at all, nor had I in the other instance when I concentrated on sending energy out.

We all had the feeling something was going for us.... It's hard to see how suggestion operated. In the aura bit, I have given myself the suggestion I'd see my own on several occasions with no effect. Florence actively fights against any suggestions, and I purposely gave none. Obviously we were trying for something—which is in itself suggestion, but on other times we've tried for example to get the table to move and it wouldn't budge. If this was the case, how come the auras were more visible in light than darkness, since you are more suggestible in the dark. The other manifestations also happened in light, though we did try darkness with no effects showing.

This is the first time literally that we've tried for any physical effects since I've steered clear of that sort of thing.

I didn't think to open my eyes to see hand bit for myself. Whether this would have broken trance or not I don't know, but as a result I saw nothing at this time; but did have the definite extension feeling on hand. Once earlier, just before, candle spurted once. Felt that energy then "leaped" to me, or that I directed it to me. Simply don't know whether any personality was present. Some thought they sensed someone. But the room <u>was</u> strange. Unstable elements I felt.

Am beginning Seth book. Yesterday told myself that all my energies physical, mental, spiritual and psychic would be released since I was doing what I was supposed to do. Any connection here?

ESP CLASS SESSION, MAY 28, 1968
TUESDAY

As old friends occasionally meet at the marketplace,

so old friends have a habit of meeting here. After some period of silence I say good evening to you all.

I am pleased that you have some good reading material for a change. We will have to see what can be done so that the practice can be continued. I am very pleased with your progress, and if I do not come through with a voice as light as a butterfly, that does not mean that I am a lightweight. I sit in on all your sessions and I am deeply amused at times, but always pleased. I have come to let you know simply that I have not deserted you. My friend here *(Rachel)* thought perhaps that I would be silent, but I cannot for long remain silent. It is simply that you must do your studying. You must concentrate and learn and I will not distract you.

It is springtime here and I hope that all your hearts are fluttering. I would give you if I could some idea to let you know that your problems are fleeting, but I can only tell you this. The feeling I cannot give you. That must be your own.

Your friend *(Anne H., speaking to Florence) is* doing well and you should not worry. I was also here last week and I am always in this room. It is very important that you read and study the material and that you not be satisfied by superficial answers and that you question, for by questioning you will learn.

I know you all very well by now. *(To Rose)* The situation in your case will work out to your advantage. I do not mean, although like Ruburt I am indeed somewhat to sound superior *[sic]*, you must however realize that you are so closely focused within the reality that you know that it is difficult for you to look elsewhere. Yet the answers are within you and you can bring them out.

I come here from a long way, but not too much is lost in the transition. There is joy also in the universe besides your problems, and the joy is paramount. Because I am the source of material I tell you: study it. There are many answers in the material that will solve or help you solve many problems that seem so difficult, but you must solve your own problems. For solving them is a challenge and helps your own development.

I see that I am greeted with long faces, long and fierce faces, and it must be a solemn occasion indeed. I should have come prepared indeed with a suitable sermon. Your friend *(Anne H.)* is happier by far now, and stronger. You only see her predicament from a limited standpoint .

... is precisely how I shall operate in the future. For I have indeed led you on in this regard, and quite cold-heartedly, for you must have your little wonders and your little spectaculars to begin with to whet your appetite. Though I am hardly spectacular, I will have to do. The material which I have given is not given in a jovial manner, even though I speak jovially at times, and for your own development it is imperative that you understand it and apply it. Like any good teacher I realize that you need incentive, and I shall supply them, and in good measure indeed. But you do not as yet know your other selves and you will meet them. Even you *(to Florence) will* meet them.

By all means continue.

([Theodore:] "About problems, I'm wondering whether to make a distinction between a problem which is a personal thing in nature that we must solve on our own, and a problem that is not so personally oriented but community oriented where the decision you have affects someone else and can be a wrong solution. And doesn't affect you personally, necessarily.")

All problems affect you personally. The community in which you live is a community which you have constructed personally. It is the en masse production that you have constructed.

Now, I speak jokingly to you, telling you that I am the origin of the material, and therefore you must listen to it and study it. The fact remains that I am also a channel through which this information comes to you. And as yet you have little idea of its significance and meaning, not only to you personally. It makes little difference that I transmit it and that Ruburt receives it. The material itself, however, is the important issue here. I receive it and interpret it from our sources, as I have told my friends. Ruburt has always been cautious here, for when I tell him of the significance of the material, then he wonders about the aspect of his own personality. But I tell you and I tell you frankly that the personality by which I show myself to you is but a small aspect of my whole personality. And that personality is not cold. You simply do not understand it, therefore I come to you in terms that you can understand, and these characteristics of mine that seem so cozy are to some extent devious. They are my characteristics as I am, but also as I was. For I am no longer what I was.

What the material tells you about the nature of your own reality is the closest you can come now to an approximation of the truth. No one, not even I, can hand you proof on a golden platter. You must understand what it is. Our beloved monster here *(the cat)* intuitively knows what is involved, and you know intuitively, but we want you to understand consciously.

Now, let you all for a moment remain quiet as I divest myself of those characteristics that you find so human and understanding, and remember that inner portions of yourselves also have existences that are as strange. Only I am aware of mine and you are not aware of yours.

(Other Personality [later named Seth II]:) I have not traveled where you are, and yet a portion of me that you know as Seth has so traveled. I am more divorced from you than he is. There is more effort involved in theses communications, for Ruburt must come farther, since I cannot come closer.

You must, you should realize, that your own personalities exist in realities of which you do not know, and yet a portion of you is so aware of these existences. You find me impersonal as Ruburt does, and yet it is simply because you do not understand the gestalt of personality and action and the meaning of identity. For my own identity is aware of many other personalities that are my own. You are also a portion of other such personalities, but egotistically you are not aware of them. Seth is a part of what I am and I know him well. It is difficult for me to explain to you what I am since the components of my reality are so different, and yet intuitively, intuitively you realize your own greater reality, and that includes the knowledge of what I am.

I come to you from a dimension which you neither know nor understand, and yet that dimension is a portion of all reality. I cannot see your own camouflaged structures clearly, I cannot perceive time, as it appears to you. I can only to some extent communicate at this channel, yet you realize that the Seth you know, while a part of my identity, is nevertheless independent, and progresses along the lines of his own development. I can impart information that is not distorted in three-dimensional terms simply because I am so apart from three-dimensional reality. On many occasions I transmit information to your Seth and he then gives it to you.

To me, your universe is perhaps as a star might appear to you. I do not perceive it clearly, but when I focus upon it, then I can perceive your psychic reality and your individual intensities. It is only the psychic distances between us that make me appear so alien to you, for my personality structure is far different from your own. I transmit information to Seth, who then interprets it for Ruburt. The information that I have would not be understandable to you in my terms, and therefore must be interpreted and translated.

I have not been [a] personality acquainted with your

own reality or with your system or with your dimension. Seth, however, has. He is therefore in a position to translate the information which I then impart. I am not in your terms male or female. These are designations that are used within your system. Seth tells me that it is difficult for you to understand this particular point.

What you experience as emotion I experience in a sort of mathematical intensity, and translate. The inner senses will help you perceive other dimensions. You will therefore not be as imprisoned within the reality that you consider ultimate. I am here simply at Seth's request to tell you that the dimension that you know is but a small spot in the all of reality, and also, that your concept of a god is highly distorted by three-dimensional concepts and ideas.

Your own reality continues, it not only involves reincarnations, but existences in other realities besides the one that you know. As the material has clearly specified, your own existence continues in probable universes along the lines charted in the inverted time theory. I have never been physical in your terms. This does not mean I am not real.

(Seth:) Nor does it mean that I am not real, you see. For both of us exist simultaneously, and other portions of your own identities exist simultaneously with those that you know. I will now let you retire to a benign and well-deserved evening rest.

ESP CLASS SESSION, MAY 30, 1968
10:10 PM THURSDAY

(This session took place at 10:10 PM on Thursday, May 30, 1968. Present were Janet Clifton and Candice.

(Part one of the session began at 10:10 and ended at 10:20.

(Seth spoke slowly, fairly deeply and fairly loudly and the voice was accompanied by the usual Seth mannerisms.)

Now. I would not think of letting you leave without giving you my greeting. You have been bugging me. Give us a moment and we shall see what we can do for you. Now... these are impressions.

1207. Three months before a proper position. I see a lower story of a house that is divided in two, it seems. An initial engagement that is not to your liking. A turnabout and another turnabout. The letters C A R which do not refer to a vehicle. A torn ligament. A marriage and to a broken strap. Five men in a group and one woman. For your friend a particularly desired, I believe, musical engagement within a three-year period. Nearly three years from this time and a connection with a woman who may help him achieve it. 1972, February perhaps a Saturday. A first child. There seems to be a woman relative, though not your mother, with whom you should use considerable care. Perhaps this is a cousin.

Now I am not going to stay with you too long since I have put my friend Ruburt through the ropes this week. But I render you my welcome and I will speak to you

SESSION 5/30/1968

again. My voice may not be melodious but I am of a sweet disposition. The classes have already indeed altered your future though you may not particularly like my saying so.

I will not introduce you to my own big brother personality this evening. Nor do I think that we should engage in any undue voice effects for my friend again will be upset due to the hour. You will have to wait for such dainties. I am indeed myself as usual however in excellent spirits and if Ruburt were not restraining me then you would not have to listen so hard to hear what I say.

(Break at 10:20. During break we discussed the above material. I am moving to California in June and now trying to get an apartment. I plan to be married in September. I assume that this is the connection with the building mentioned and the three months prior to a proper position. The letters C A R are part of the last name of a person I was thinking about prior to the session and this could be the reference. My friend as referred to in the session is the one I plan to marry in September. He is a musician and now forming a group. Jane knew vaguely of this but did not know that he now has a torn ligament and must wear some kind of waist brace that I don't know the technical name for but I always call it a strap. The material mentions 6 group members and this is what he hopes for but doesn't have the 6 people yet. I am at present at odds with my aunt, a female relative, and I know I should be handling this situation better.

(I believe Janet was the one who is referred to in this note. This appears to be the last ESP class session she attended.)

(Jane continued at 10:25.)

Now I thought I would give you some goodies in reward for reading so much of the material. You must be more cautious with the relative I mentioned. There are influences working and she could cause you to return when you do not want to through influencing your parent. You should be diplomatic for this could occur three or four months after you arrive at your destination.

Now send me a postcard. You had better send it to Ruburt however. We will have some talks together when the hour is earlier and my keeper here is not watching after me so carefully. It is truly a pity where I feel so well to be so restrained. My friend has his problems and I would not want him put out of his comfortable shelter so that I would have to speak from the middle of a rainy field.

(10:30.)

ESP CLASS SESSION, JUNE 4, 1968
TUESDAY

Do not go, for these ... I will wait for your toy.
([Theodore:] "Thank you.")

I should not say this, but since I am with friends, I shall. Simple things amuse simple minds. You understand, I know, that I mean it well, for I understand the necessity for records, and I would not have it that this voice of mine should go unrecorded and seep into the walls.

My friend here *(Rachel)* was ready to leave. I did not think it would be dignified of me to grab her by the dress collar and to bring her back. Last week and this week I am coming through, but then there will be again a period of study. I come through to encourage you. I could have waited until our friend here was at the front door, and yelled with Ruburt's lungs to call her back. My keeper here would not permit it, however.

Now there have been several developments here in class with these two *(Vera and Theodore)* and there are other developments which should come in this class. And before I speak to you again, I expect to see that these developments have, indeed occurred. And when I pat you on the back you will know.

I told you that the affair would work out well *(Rose)* and you can, I believe, expect further developments during the next ten days in particular. Doctors and teachers get along well, you see. We are the professional elite, like yourselves indeed.

I have been here, as Ruburt knows well, through your class this evening, and he has given me permission, for I would not dare peek into this class unless he told me that I could do so. For such a small and slender snip he holds his own. We do, however, have a very good relationship, as I'm sure you know by now. And you understand, I know, my humor. My energy has been silent but potent in this room, like that bottle of wine that sits upon the table. But Ruburt knew that I would be here before class was over, and I come to you with no great pronouncements. The material is my pronouncement, and I back up the material with my presence. And when you read the material, then indeed you know who it is that has given it, and if you hear a laugh behind the material as you read it, let there be no doubt in your mind that I am here. While I do not follow you, tippety-toe, behind you to your school halls and your hallowed bank corridors, nevertheless I am aware, generally, of your activities, and I know when you are reading my material.

When I come in this class I do so so that you realize the knowledge that is in the material comes through a personality, and that I am not some "ditto." I have been here emotionally, hardly hidden in the folds of the curtains. I want you to realize that the material has been sifted through my experience. That the words are not dead, as indeed I am far from dead. A livelier spirit you have never encountered! The material, in other words, is given by me, a living personality, to you, and you are living personalities. We dwell in different dimensions but vitality and personality dwell in all dimensions. This room is saturated with my presence as if you had sprinkled it with that heady wine, aged wine. Indeed, I do not find it remarkable that you consider me a personality since, indeed that is what I am. Nor do I find it remarkable that you were not frightened. I do not consider myself a frightening phenomenon. Indeed, I find some of you much more frightening. I enjoy sitting here quietly, picking up your thoughts.

([Theodore:] "That goes double" [to Rachel]; "Spare me" [to Seth].)

I need not spare you, spare yourself, young man. Your many individual thoughts blend for me. I know where they are coming from, but they blend into not too harmonious an orchestra. I am not musically inclined, however.

One remark, I did not mean to imply that I had any hand at all in the healing process to which I referred earlier. My methods are my methods, and I do not believe in shortcuts. However, shortcuts are taken, and I have no disagreement with the methods of others. I am aware of them, and I am pleased that the process has begun. I am aware that the process has begun and I am aware of what is being done. I am a harder teacher. I am not taking credit, you see, for another man's abilities. I am much more interested, unfortunately, in the more painful process involved in self-realization, spiritual insight, and psychological knowledge. I would demand that your husband know why *(to Rose)* and rid himself of the problem that was causing the symptoms. To relieve the symptoms is indeed pleasant, and human, and understandable. And I have no quarrel with this. But it is far more important to understand why you are creating a distortion in physical reality that concerns your own image. For the problem must be solved now or later. It is possible that the relief of symptoms will lead to psychological and spiritual regeneration, in which case it is doubly and triply beneficial. But problems within a personality and *[sic]* itself will manifest itself in one way or another unless the problem itself is solved.

(V. whispered to T. asking if he was watching the tape.) I sipsise (?) *[sic]* whispers. I should perhaps address myself here, to this toy. I should forget you all and speak to it so that my tones may then be immortalized forever. My tones are indeed immortalized forever, but your tones are also immortalized forever. And this is what you must realize and understand, for if my presence permeates this room, so does your combined presence permeate this room and any room in which you have lived.

Although I speak to you rather slowly this evening and regrettably without any words of profound weight, nevertheless I am with you more closely this evening than I have been in any other session, but I shall not give you the privilege of hearing my clear, birdlike tones until you have done more work. This does not only mean reading the material. It means the work involved in looking into yourselves. I cannot do this for you, and no one can do it for you, and no one can make you do it before you yourself are ready to look into the meaning of your own existence and your own personality.

I could, I could put you *(Florence)* into a trance such as few have been in before. It is an easy road, and my methods are not easy. Your own ego and consciousness must learn and develop and not be coerced into any kind of submission, for you would resent it, as indeed I would resent and coercion.

We have here in the room unbeknown to all of you

a perpetual motion machine *(Rachel swinging her leg)*. This leg here.

Now when I speak to you as I have this evening, my purpose, my one and main purpose, is to let you sense the endless vitality that is mine, though you, in conventional terms, would designate me by some ridiculous word—survival personality, as Ruburt says, or "spirit" or "dead." My vitality is the same vitality that is your own. I am not here, in your terms, but I am very much here.

There was some definite information I wanted to give to you, which I have given. If my friend here would permit it, and he will not, I could easily shatter the glass of the window with as little effort as is required for a child to breathe. Far be it for me to give such childish demonstrations.

(As Jane threw her glasses on the floor, going into her third trance of the evening, Theodore said, "I'm going to catch that some day.")

Are you ready?

([Theodore:] "Yes, man.")

There is some understandable confusion there. Now, to end the suspense I will indeed shortly say good evening to you *(after each previous trance we wondered if Seth would be back, since he hadn't said good night, and he always says good night)*. Well, I am here, indeed I am here, and if you want to think of me as some UFO *(earlier talking about someone mailing a card to Robbie, Jane and Seth, what or how would they address it)*, that is your privilege. When Ruburt receives my energy, often he does not know what to do with it. It radiates out from that small frame. He thinks that the energy collects about him until it could shatter the walls of the room. I can see the timbers falling upon your heads. A timberhead.

([Theodore:] "A knucklehead."

He is learning to contain and focus the energy that is mine. Would you prefer that I be as silent and solitary and quiet as a tiny pin that sits upon the blue rug? I can prick you all indeed and cut you up. Only because I make you think, do not ever believe that I would have you forget your banking *[sic]* intellect, for this is not the case, and if there is much I have not said to you, it is because you know already what I would say to you. I want you to realize that all personality exists beyond what you call the grave, and that what I am has been here in many guises, as indeed, so have you. And that the personal characteristics by which I have been known continue.

But the other personality that you find so alien is also my own. And the familiarity and the very human characteristics by which you know me are mine, but they are only a small portion of my identity. The energy that is used as I speak to you can be utilized in many ways, and the energy that is yours can be utilized in many ways. Watch the ways you utilize your energy. It goes forth from you and you do not realize consciously how it is going forth and what it is doing. This energy is a protection of your own personality and your own will and of your own spirit. Every man and woman has protection. Your astro-body *[sic]* is to some extent a projection and a protection. Do not be afraid of vitality nor of your own feeling. Others are protected from your own feeling, as you are protected to a large extent from theirs.

I should be a bishop, for the looks upon your faces, the reverence and the quiet and the awed expression. I am indeed honored. I feel, and I do indeed feel, as you with the perpetual motion leg will know, like a friend to all of you this evening and hardly like a bishop. Nor would I think of shattering a window to prove so paltry a point as the existence of my own unlimited vitality and energy. For my friend Ruburt would never allow it. However, my thoughts are strong. My only point in such unseeming *[sic]* and undignified, unbusinesslike and unconventional demonstration—I would make a poor bank president—my only point is to let you know that existence knows no barriers and a breeze and ease through blood and bone are born *[sic]*. I could and I would—and I would—enjoy speaking in such a manner until dawn, but you could never take it, and Ruburt would hide in the cellar for three days following.

Know, however, that your own emotions and your own feeling and your own vitality has such an energy and a power as my voice shows this evening. And it is your purpose to utilize and direct and focus your own energy. Ruburt is speaking for me—why do you cough *(Rose)*? Do not look so upset and embarrassed.

Now, only because of the hour and Ruburt constant(ly) probing which I do indeed feel, I will leave you, and it will indeed be some classes before I return, for you have your own problems to consider, your own inner development to consider.

And if I did not welcome you suitably, I do so now *(to Candice)*.

So I tell you, to end the everlasting suspense—my friends, good evening and good night.

I will be here, I will be silent for a change. If you miss your classes, I will know it. And I may indeed choose to speak precisely when you do not come, for I am sly. And to get my material across, and to get you to develop, I use many educational aids.

ESP CLASS SESSION, AUGUST 20, 1968
TUESDAY

I am no Volkswagen, that I am waiting for you. First of all, you must forget words like purpose and time. For as you have learned, they will impede your progress. They are limiting words. We shall give you better ones. I shall have to make up a dictionary for you. I will give you a vocabulary test. Pronunciation, meaning and spelling. Now as far as possible, you should divest yourselves of words that limit your concept. You must pretend that you are learning a new language and indeed you are. The language with which we are working, however, deals with far more than words. We must use words as you are aware of them. The words are all that shows, but beneath those words are actualities and realities. We can only hint at these with the use of words, and this is why we must be very careful as to which words we use. We must be very choosy and I know indeed that you are all very choosy people since you are here.

You are each a center and a focus point and an individuality, and around you are circling realities and you have an existence in each of these. The inner self is aware, but the conscious self is not aware. It seems to you as you read the session that you are small and tiny, with reality spinning about you that you can neither see nor understand, but this is not the case, for a part of you does know. You are a part of these encircling realities and your dreams and thoughts and wishes affect those realities even though you are not consciously aware of this. And when you pluck a finger into the air, then you disturb and change and alter other realities that you cannot see nor touch, and other realities in which a finger, as a finger, does not exist. One thought sends out ripples that change and alter. One of your own dreams rising out from you as its center, it touches and changes these other realities. There is no feeling that you have, there is no word that you utter, there is no thought hidden in the deepest environment of your brain that does not have a reality different than the one you know. That does not reach out and change and grow and alter worlds of which you have no knowledge.

So do not feel that you are powerless, do not feel that you are at the mercy of events, for you form events not only in this reality, but in these other realities which you do not consciously understand. Each move that you make is not multiplied a million times, not simply multiplied, but it reaches out and changes and alters and affects these other realities and it becomes a new action. It becomes a new action as it approaches and reaches other realities, and it in turn initiates action. For it will meet with responses, and these responses will be different. There is nothing that goes on in this room when you are here that goes on in this room alone. These meetings occur in this room, but they also occur in other realities, and when you come here to this class you are also attending a class on another level, and you are not aware of those classes, though I am aware of them. I am very aware of them, for while our friend Ruburt gives this class, I have been giving other classes and you have all been there. Education takes place on many levels.

A portion of yourselves exist also in many other realities. When these classes in this room are in progression, other portions of your own personality are attending other classes. You are fairly decent students on all levels, though I have not given you an A—that is because I am a difficult teacher. Now. This is an analogy—replicas of this room containing each of you exists now as you think of now in many other realities. Ruburt will explain electrical reality from our sessions. He will explain probabilities to you from our sessions. And you will see that while you are aware of simply one room and one time, and one evening and one class in your present moment, there are other rooms and other classes and you sit in them all. And each of you are given information according to the developments and characteristics of that particular portion of yourself who is attending.

In your terms, you are hanging out in space with nothing to support you and our friend here would be terrified of falling. You know that the physical floor does not support you, but you must pretend that the physical floor supports you or you would be dizzier than you are. So also at this moment in other realities do you sit, replicas of yourselves in other rooms and in other classes. And each moment as you know it, with this activity as you know it, exists in other realities, and you are a portion of these realities and you affect them. As you go out and speak to others now, and change them, so on other levels do you do the same, and so indeed are you also changed and affected.

This room could disconnect itself from this apartment building and go sailing blithely through space. And yet under many circumstances you would not be aware of it, for within the room if it sailed about evenly, the perspective would still be the same. And unless you looked out of the windows you would notice no change. But if the windows were sealed and closed, you would not know the difference, and so until you learn to look out of the windows to the inner selves, then you will not realize what your own environment consists of. For the perspective where you look is the same, and you have nothing to judge experience against. I will let my friend here take a break. He is broken up because he has moved his furniture, but he does not confuse me.

(Seth withdrew and there was a class break.)

You could call me a transplant. My heart would not do anyone much good, however, for you could not find it. There are many reasons, and all highly individual reasons, why various people choose different methods of death. There is no one reason, there is no one answer to any such question. There will be, however, a characteristic way of dying that will be adapted by different personalities. The ego may be strong enough to hold the whole personality back. The earthly temperament may simply hold on. The inner self in many instances will go ahead and wait.

There is a consciousness within the atoms and molecules that compose the body. There is also a group consciousness that is made up. It is a combination. You may call it a nature consciousness. There is no strongly organizing principle behind it. It is the overall consciousness composed of the atoms and molecules within the physical structure and when the main personality has gone its way, this simple consciousness may persist for some time. Even this however will withdraw. In many instances, however, this simple consciousness will be retained for some time, in your terms. It is this portion that belongs rather closely to your own. It is this consciousness that is the simple source of your physical apparatus. It is this consciousness that has been formed particularly within your system from each cell. The individual consciousness of it will withdraw from each atom and molecule within the physical body. Each minute consciousness will withdraw.

You can compare these to simple earth spirits, but

they are aware. They will in turn inhabit other forms, and even the most minute consciousness that resides within the smallest portion of matter, even that consciousness can grow and mature and change, for there is no limitation set upon consciousness. Even then, the smallest consciousness within its own terms of value fulfillment can emerge, can change, can alter, can develop. It can then gain and gather about it the potentiality to hold and control more and more energy. It can broaden the apparent boundaries of its own existence, for all boundaries are only apparent. They are illusions. Even the boundaries that you set about your own identities are illusions. They are not solid. You can go beyond them. It is difficult to portray to you the complexity of the realities themselves. For the difficult realm *[sic]* cannot understand the concepts that are involved.

You mentioned something earlier in class. Now indeed, not only does each thought have an electrical reality of its own and endures unchanged, but what you consider to be yourself has an electrical reality and is coded in terms that you cannot presently understand. We have explained this in various past sessions. There is individual consciousnesses can also merge with others *[sic]*. When this occurs no individuality is ever lost, but each of *(the)* joining consciousnesses are able to participate in greater realities. Now, I will not keep you too long this evening, but it is too long since I have been here to keep you on your toes.

Bega is doing well in his classes, and you are doing

well in these classes. You are all developing and growing, whether or not you are consciously aware of it, and when you gather together there are beneficial developments that you do not understand, and that I am not prepared to explain to you this evening, for it would take too much of your time. There is, however, a pooling of inner knowledge that is highly helpful to all of you. I do not expect you to drown in that pool, for I have taught you how to swim, you see. And take care that you look out of the windows now and then, lest you all go sailing past West Water Street.

Jewel and I will polish you up. Now, all you need do is imagine I am speaking to you and you will go to sleep nights, since I seem to have that effect upon you in class. I am not a sandman. In case you are curious, in your particular case there is a relaxation of the nervous system that occurs, but not because of my melodious tones, I will note, but indeed my voice can travel as far as the onions *[sic!]*.

I did not say good evening to you, and so I now do so. I give you again what blessings are mine to give and I will return to classes often. And often when you do not expect me.

ESP CLASS SESSION, SEPTEMBER 17, 1968
TUESDAY

A quieter bunch I have never seen! I dare not keep my friend Ruburt too long, for I have put him through his paces this week indeed. And we have been conversing with people of some note—I was on my good manners. We have indeed seriously made some good friends. But there are no friends like old friends and no lights like lights that explode. I could not have you so maligned. Obviously I was not annoyed. I was amused, and my amusement on occasions takes odd form.

I still do not understand, however, why earlier Ruburt whispered and why these long serious faces as we sit about the table. You must not project your own feelings at this point upon others. The dead are not long-faced. Why should they come into such a long-faced sober group?

Now if I were coming here for fun, I would indeed enjoy smiles and light and conversation. I would not, however, think of coming to such a sober group for fun. I had indeed better put on my *(words lost)* and instruct you.

I did, as always, have a purpose this evening in making myself known. And if now and then I indulge in a few very human reactions, then you must forgive me. But the matter, the lights, did indeed seem a suitable reaction on my part. I enjoyed it.

Now in time, you will all receive individual sessions, and in time you will receive enough individual sessions so that you will have something upon which to build. And then I may not be so jovial. I am glad at least to see some smiles and broad ones, and laughter. We are, in many cases you understand, more jovial than you, for we can see the humor where in many cases you can not.

I will not again, since I have put Ruburt through so much this week, I will not speak loudly. There was another point, however, that I wanted to make, and I have spoken to you many times to get this simple point across, and yet by your actions this evening, all of you then, I can see that I have not put that point across. I will mention it again.

<u>All</u>, <u>all</u>—life is full of vitality, and all life is joyful, and sitting around the table with long faces is not any more beneficial than sitting around the table with wine on it and the lights lit. My vitality is here, and it was not drawn here by long faces nor by sorrow. Vitality grows as it triumphs over sorrows and in any of my antics, as with the suddenly exploding light, there is also a purpose. And the purpose in that point was to let you see that the human individual reaction of a given personality continues. Only those very sure of their reality can afford to take pleasure in small things and to enjoy them.

Now I shall keep silent for a while. But I have been here this evening and I will be here a while longer. And I shall leave the light where it belongs.

(Break.)

I did not realize that Ruburt was such a taskmaster. I shall speak to him about it on your behalf.

SESSION 9/17/1968

([Theodore:] "Crack the whip!")

Someone *(Theodore)* over there seems too anxious. I do welcome you *(Zen Dean)* to this room.

Now you should feel a strong vitality here, and you should feel it touch each of you. You all have a vitality and energy that you do not realize that you possess, and it takes such an ancient, old decrepit, sorrowful spirit such as I to tell you. The energy used in this room this evening and in your talk and chatter, that energy barely touches upon the energy that you have and that you have not yet directed.

Now it is well and good for me to come here. You need not think any of this reprimand for you. It is fine and well for me to come here and talk to you, but you are not taking time from your daily activities to develop your own abilities, not to look inward, and you *(Theodore)* need not be included here. You will have your sessions when you take some time to look within yourselves. You must do part of your own work. I shall not do it for you. I even make Ruburt do his own work and I ride him hard. For I am also some taskmaster, but you must be your own taskmasters also.

There is a door within yourselves and you know that it exists. And you have your hand upon the knob. You will not get an electric shock when you touch it. You have merely to look within yourselves and open the door. You have merely to take some time for peace and quiet amid the objective activities of your day. There is nothing for you to fear behind that door. The both of you *(Sally and*

Florence) hide fear behind different faces. Behind that door lies spontaneity and joy and understanding, and from these you have nothing to fear.

You know you have nothing to fear, but you do not know what you have to gain. You have much to gain. The momentary fear that you have felt was nothing, and it was not symbolic of a deeper, different fear. You need concentration and focus and a strong impetus, and you can develop these and use them. You *(Rachel)* have also the fear, but it is a superficial one and can be overcome. But these things require that you look inward. That within your activities you find a period of peace.

Once you've touched the doorknob and once you turn it, the energy and vitality and freedom that you will feel will overwhelm you, and make your daily lives more vital, and you can use your energies and direct them. A thousand situations that seem willy-nilly will make sense to you and you can deal with them.

Now I have the serious faces. As our new friend would say, "Now we are getting down to the nitty-gritty." This is your life, and your life, and your life, and not mine. While I can offer suggestions and impetus, there is no one that can open that door but yourself. You have found the door, you have beat aside the jungles of repressions *(words lost)* door.

Now that I have taken you all down a peg, remember, there is no grade behind that door. There is only freedom and strength and joy and vitality. I can poke your arm so that you move the knob a bit, but that is all that I can do. You can open the door and I am indeed sure that you will do so. I am also sure that a little talk like this will help you do so quicker. Now, I will cease, and whether or not I shall speak again this evening, who of you knows?

(Break.

(Florence has been typing the Seth sessions for us.)

You *(Florence)* cannot get indulgences from me, you see, for this—"quote." I appreciate the effort and I thank you, but for your own development, you must still look inward.

I played with the light to help you out. The work that you *(Florence)* have done here helps all of the students and it does help you, but you must still open the door. The doorknob works, it will not fall off in your hands. The door will not explode and you have nothing to fear. If I could give you indulgences then I would.

I will have more to say in your *(Sally)* case also. For again the fear is there. And you try. You try to tint the fears with smiles, you try to pat it as you would a dog in hopes that it will not bite *(words lost)* you. But you do not understand the fear, and therefore you do not know how to speak its language, and when it speaks to you, you do not understand it. You can conquer the fear, but you must understand it. Give us a moment here. The fear will not devour you. You have given it fantastic proportions. You have exaggerated its strength, and because you have exaggerated its strength, you have given it more strength than it possesses on its own. You also fear to open the door.

Do not pretend that the fear does not exist.

Recognize it simply, it will then lose much of its charge. This is the first step in ridding yourself of it.

If a dark angry mongrel follows you down the street and you know it and you say to yourself, "It is a fine day and I am alone and there is no dog behind me," and it yaps at your feet and you say, "It is a lovely day and no dog yaps at my feet," and it growls at your ankles and you run as fast as you can saying all the time, "Nothing chases me," and you dare not look back; then in your mind the dog springs from a dog to a tiger, to an unnamable terror. And you do not look around to see that it is merely a small dog, but in your mind you build these fears. If you stop and turn around to see what is bothering you and you find a small dog, then you take a deep breath of relief and wish you had turned around sooner. This is you *(Sally)* and your fear.

ESP CLASS SESSION, OCTOBER 8, 1968 TUESDAY

You will forgive me if I do not attend that particular class. Now, I have been a liberal from way back, and yet there are certain circumstances indeed where I become very conservative. To take my clothes off and end up with a woman's body—there indeed I draw the line! Now as you have known, I have been here this evening, bell and all. If I occasionally take you to task, I am speaking to two members of the class in particular, and if I occasionally take you to task, then ask yourselves who else cares enough to take you to task, and if I do not take you to task, who else will take you to task? When I give A's they are well earned.

I welcome back our world traveler, and when you are a space and time traveler as well, then I shall also welcome you back. You all travel far beyond the confines of the world that you think you know, and you waken in the morning with little memory of where you have been. And here we have a traveler indeed, for you travel further than most, but you do not want to remember. That is perfectly all right, you go where you go and you travel where you travel, and if you want to tear your tickets up in the morning and forget where you have been, that is your own privilege.

(To Theodore) We know of course this Bega—and he is trained to do a fairly decent job with you and you are a fairly good student. You must learn, however, to forget the world that you know physically. When you are working with Bega you must try to let down and forget your physical data, for you do not know him well enough yet. You do not let him come through clearly enough. But he shall in time, and you will recognize the difference.

I have spoken to our Lady of Florence over there on several occasions, in the dream state, since she will not hear me any other way. And I have spoken clearly, as indeed is my way. And we have played question and answer games. You know now, I do not have to tell you, that you are not actuating all your abilities. You are not using them to your benefit. Now you are in too many places at once. You do not concentrate on one thing at a time. It will not be too difficult for you to develop your abilities, but it will be difficult for you to learn the self-discipline that is necessary. You can learn self-discipline, and I will be a taskmaster.

I will let our friend take a rest. Your thoughts buzz about like a bee *(rings bell)*. Now you may take a rest and then I shall call the class to order *(ringing bell)*, and my kind of order...

And I drank brandy in my day and it was not hidden in tiny chocolate boxes...

Now I ring the bell—and I will clear up a slight issue that has come to my attention. Your teacher, your immediate teacher, has had strong creative abilities and he was very jealous as to how they should be used. He would set the conditions. He would use them in such and such a manner and no other. Now you should realize that this endeavor is indeed a highly creative one, for you have here at the least, at the very least, two personalities, my own and Ruburt's, and we dwell entirely *(in)* different dimensions. And the mode of communication must be set up between us if what I want to say will be said.

Now you hear the words, but I am behind the words and highly creative activities must go on on both our parts, so that my thoughts can be translated into words that will make meaning and sense to you. I must transform certain mechanisms within Ruburt's physical mechanisms. I must play upon them as a painter plays with color or a musician plays with notes and keys, and he

(Ruburt) must acquiesce and join in this creative activity. Then in his books he must further use his creative ability to translate what I have said. We use Ruburt's nervous mechanism and we change it creatively, as to a lesser extent we hope to change you all creatively.

Now, I did not speak earlier, and I have not spoken directly before to Lafinda, and Lafinda is the entity name for Vera. Now, it is she who provides strongly a supportive atmosphere in which you work. It is she who provides the warm spontaneity that allows you to develop. She knows and consciously does not realize she knows. She provides steps of energy that allow you to move upwards, she provides strength when you need it.

Give us a moment here…

There is energy within her that is given gladly and is used by the entire physical family. As long as she is certain of your loyalty and support, then she is a firm foundation upon which you may all build. Now, there is something here upon which I shall not dwell in class. —The wine is not as good as the brandy! —However, I will say here that large portions of her energy are diverted to provide supportive help physically for all members of the family. She is not religiously inclined in your terms because she does not need religion in those terms. She is intuitively aware of her position with All That Is, and she does not need to rationalize it.

For your information I can taste the wine and fortunately I am not affected by the wine, although Ruburt may be.

Now. Our Lady of Florence, it is true that if you go outward and up you will find an inwardness, but this is not the easiest way to go about it. They also serve who only stand and wait. They serve mightily who serve up copies of the nature of physical matter. The effort, again, is highly appreciated, very highly. But you cannot bribe yourself, much less me. One of these days you will have to look inward. There is no other way, and all ways lead to that way.

I will ring my bell and awaken our friend and if you can hear it, then I can hear it and I will return if you promise to give Ruburt no more rumolade in candies. If you are as lively as I am at my age, then you can indeed sing hosannas...

All right now, I will fix all of you. I will say good evening to you now, but I will continue what I have to say when you go to sleep this evening. I will continue my dissertation, for I had one planned. If you will not listen to me when you are awake because it is too late, then I shall be like a recording machine so that you learn while you sleep. I may indeed take care of you *(to Theodore)*. Joking aside, I will speak to those now here this evening while you sleep, and you may ask me what questions you have. You may or may not remember. Over that I have no control, and it goes without saying that you can listen or not. I will not force, and would not force, myself upon you. But you are not sufficiently impressed with the reality of your existence within the dream state. You still do not realize its significance. You still do not realize the potential that you have and that you use in the dream state, and that you do not use ordinarily in your waking life. Now when I speak to you, you may remember me, but you may very well see me as you think I am.

Now I give you all again those blessings that are mine to give, and I am here with you very clearly this evening so that you should be able rather vividly to sense my reality, and in sensing my reality to sense that greater reality of your own. So though I say good evening to you now, I will visit again with you whether or not you remember, for a portion of you will know, and the portion of you never forgets such encounters.

It is only because I am so aware of the reality of time to you that I leave now, for I realize that your hour is late. But time is as transparent as the air in this room and your 8, 9, 10, 11, 12 o'clock flies through the air like birds. I speak to you all individually and individually you all know me, so while you all hear the same words individually they mean something different to each of you.

I give you then my heartiest good wishes, and we shall continue our discussion when you have gone beddy-bye. Instead of visions of sugar plums I shall dance within your heads! Now, I am quite prepared to continue quite as I am now with you here for some time. It is only out of the goodness of my invisible heart and my sympathy and understanding for your human conditions that I hereby say, temporarily, good evening.

ESP CLASS SESSION, OCTOBER 22, 1968
TUESDAY

I am at the hub of your group and draw you together. Our friend here *(Jane)* had some experience last evening so I will not keep him overlong. He has been impatient with you and I have been impatient with him for being impatient with you. The teachers squabble over their methods and the cats will play.

Now, all of you gather strength when you are here and you use it in your own ways. The place is like a touchstone. You are afraid to touch it too much for fear of getting burned and I know this. You want to know but not too much too fast. I know this and it does not bother me so I don't see why it should bother our friend *(Ruburt)* here.

I have, to some extent, your histories before me and I see your giant steps and your tiny steps and I see where you trip. I am behind you in the dark and I give you a push when it is needed—not a hard push—a nudge. Ruburt would indeed push you and shove you.

Now, your candle episode was legitimate. It was not some breeze playfully passing by. Now I am a big wind playfully passing by. The candle was moved. The flame was moved, if my friend Ruburt will forgive me, by a friendly spirit who was within call. I can't understand why he did not know the message was received.

Now, you are together in ways you do not understand. Someday I will explain them. You have come here for your own reasons and though you should know what your reasons are, someday I will tell you.

Now, your autumn comes. Let it remind you that all things within your system sleep and then awaken, and that jokes constantly told, are no longer funny. They must lie in wait for a while and then reincarnate—spring up anew. True jokes are mysteries and are not jokes as you understand them.

Now, although I admit I usually come to you with a voice like a musical thunder, with a voice that seems to weigh a thousand pounds, that seems to plop into the room, yet I can also come lightly as a leaf and be here when you do not know. *(Florence tried to smother a cough and Seth boomed out.)* You may cough to your heart's content. You may all cough and have a coughing session!!

Now, all of you will get your precious reincarnational data in one way or another. I will let my friend take his break.

(Seth withdrew. During break, Florence brought up the question of the will of God—whether God has control over what happens to us, etc. Seth suddenly spoke:)

<u>No</u> stimuli is ever accidental. No stimuli is <u>ever</u> accidental. I repeat the sentence so you can understand it. You are never controlled. God is creativity and he creates creativity or other creators. Creativity of necessity, because of its nature, leads to further development and existence—to further creations. Control leads to rigidity, nonexistence and the negation of all. In the terms that are usually used, perfection would be death and annihilation, for it presup-

poses an end beyond which no progress is possible. Creativity always knows that further development always lies latent. New possibilities grow constantly from the heart and spirit. To control is to court rigidity. No God knows the word or the meaning of control, nor does he exert control as far as his abilities are concerned, for it would lead to dead alleys, and spirituality would go and leave him dried up as a fruit pit.

It is not my ego that remains, for I have shed egos as a snake sheds skin. It is my <u>identity</u> that remains and it is <u>your</u> identity that remains. Freedom knows its own control, but not the kind you are thinking of. Spontaneity, indeed, has its own discipline and is never applied from without. It is the other side of the coin. There is no such control, then. Spontaneity knows its own direction and the god is not fearful. Control is a result of fear.

(Seth withdrew, and as break was starting and Jane began coming out of trance, Florence, shaking her fingers after writing for so long, made a comment that she wished the tape recorder was here. Seth immediately broke back in.)

I can play whether or not your toy is playing. You have your own tape recorder within your mind and you will remember what I said.

Now, do not walk so heavily the paths of earth. Walk lightly. The weight you carry is not physical. It is not physical pounds that weigh you down. Your own identities will enlighten you. There is no need for you to concentrate so avidly and exclusively upon the physical paths. You have walked other paths.

You *(this seemed directed to Rachel)* have cultivated other gardens. There are joys that can lighten your burden. It is not your ego that you fight, although you have a model of an ego. You fight a memory that lingers on the outskirts of your mind. A transgression already forgiven—a storm already passed—a dark cloud already punctured. Now, you are naturally as free as air. The rest is a facade to hide the memory. Now, consciously you will not understand what I am telling you but unconsciously you will. The transgression has already been paid for. The penance is finished. When you realize that you are free you will be able to enjoy your freedom.

Now what brings you here? Knowledge that you do not realize that you possess, yet you do possess it. I look back again at your past histories and to your probabilities and futures in your terms, and my, how you change. You would not know yourselves. Be good of heart. You have more staying power than you know and you *(Amelia)* should realize that you are also here for a reason and that you build more that garden roads.

There is no reason to fear your inner selves. It is to your inner selves that I speak. They will not betray you, only betray you with truth and that is an honor indeed. The light will not blind your eyes but open new eyes you do not know you possess, give you freedom you do not know... Only truth will give you a sense of humor.

Now, if you will not break into many pieces, you may take your break—the clatter of pieces crashing to the floor would tax Ruburt's new vacuum sweeper—or tax fingers that are breaking with fatigue.

(Seth withdrew and there was a class break.)

Now that was a fine sermon and I shall take it to heart. The barriers that you erect are no longer needed. The dangers have long since passed. They have been conquered. The transgressions were not as severe as your strong conscious supposed and the time of penance is over.

(Sally softly cleared her throat.) A polite cough, indeed. Now were I a kind and well-known beloved uncle who has passed over, you could perchance see me, but for now you must be content with the little of me that I am able to portray through Ruburt's personality. There should be occasions when Ruburt's features will change to some considerable extent when I speak to you, but you will have to be content for now with that part of me you can sense. You will perceive more of me as time goes by. I will not come playing hopscotch, jumping through the window like Peter Pan. It is not my style. But I tell you that you will perceive me more clearly than you do now.

I will even sometimes wander. Be quite assured that I will keep my eyes, figuratively speaking, upon you although I am not Big Brother spying upon your activities. But I know when you wander from your purpose and when you leap spontaneously toward it and when in the depths of your being you realize the depths of your abilities and deny them.

Now discipline is knowing how to use spontaneity and only the fear of blessed spontaneity brings sadness,

SESSION 10/22/1968

for it impedes progress and puts boulders in your path. Step lightly. You leap from truth to truth. Truths are not heavy. They are light. They are light in weight and in illumination. They fill you without effort. Truth keeps you sitting upright in your chairs and the blood pounding in your veins and allows me to come to this room. If you hide behind a tree in a game of hide and seek, then truth is the tree. It is <u>you</u> who think you hide, for it is a part of you and all that you are. It is you as much as it is me and it is abundant and spontaneous and is not controlled.

(Seth withdrew. Jane seemed to have a hard time coming out of trance and Sally touched her shoulder and said, "Jane, are you coming back?" Seth came through abruptly.)

I am coming back! Now I will not keep you. When you want to try psy-time, think of me. Think of the small sphere upon which you have placed yourself and that you form it, the world and everything that you know, from within—and that the truths will come from within and not from without. Imagine the sun as being within you as indeed it is, and feel it shine through the seemingly boundless boundaries of your being.

For if you listen inwardly, you can hear the first words spoken upon your planet. You can hear the yawn from Rachel that fills this so quiet room. You can hear the first breath and the last breath that will be breathed in your terms upon this planet. You have only to close your eyes and look inward. You have only to realize that truth is a joyful thing and not to be feared. You have only to realize that all the time is within you now. You have only to close your eyes and see—as now, if all of you are quiet you can feel the cosmic breezes blow through your cheeks, and yesterday flies through your skull like clouds disappearing. You have only to recognize the creativity within yourself. You have only to listen to your creative drive within you. For as surely as you sit and exist in this room, you exist beyond this room. When you go to sleep, you are free.

You *(to Amelia)* may take your leave. You do not need to raise your hand.

I wish you a hearty good evening.

ESP CLASS SESSION, DECEMBER 10, 1968 TUESDAY

This is for you (to *Florence).*

Identity is not the same thing as personality. Personality is that part of identity that manifests itself within physical reality and within your time. Identity is far greater than personality. Personality represents only those aspects of identity that you are able to actualize within three-dimensional existence. The inner self knows who it is. The inner self communicates with your present personality. In your dreams you have communication with that larger portion of yourself that is your identity. Personality may be to some extent molded by circumstance. Identity uses the experiences. Identity is not carried willy-nilly, but holds its own.

If you had read more of the material and if you had studied the information more carefully on action and identity, then you would know what I mean. You can consider the whole self as an onion if you wish. There are layers and layers and layers, but these layers all grow from the inside outward as though the inner identity forms layers and layers of personality. These personalities are part of the identity but not the entire identity.

It is true there are no limitations to the self, and in one respect you can say that the self reaches out and encompasses the environment. Current feelings regarding personality, however, do not take into consideration the existence of telepathy or clairvoyance, nor the fact of reincarnation. And so what you have, in effect, as I have said often before, is a one-dimensional psychology. You need a multi-dimensional psychology for identity operates in many dimensions beside a physical one. If you examine your own dreams, you know that for yourself. Now, that is for your record.

Now, for your class! You have here a provocative study or demonstration in the nature of personality for your club. For my personality is not Ruburt, nor is Ruburt mine. We even have the words of a signed psychologist saying that I am not a secondary personality. I make no attempt to dominate Ruburt's private life nor, indeed would I expect him to allow it. There are no points of conflict. I do not represent any restrained or any inhibited portions of Ruburt's own being. As you all know, he is hardly the inhibited type on his own! I have helped him in that his personality operates more effectively. He is able to use his ability more fully. But that it seems so could hardly be psychological crime.

The facts are, dear psychology class and professor, that _all_ of you are more than you know and that personality and identity are far different than you usually believe. Although each of you realizes privately the truth, and the truth is not easy to put into words, no one can do more than approximate it. However, each of you exists in other realities and other dimensions, and the selves that you call yourself is but a small portion of your own I.

Now while you dream, you _do_ have contact with other portions of yourselves. But while you are awake this communication also goes on continually but you are not aware of it, for your ego is so focused upon physical reality and upon survival within it, that you do not allow yourself to listen to the inner voice.

If you think of yourselves honestly and deeply when you are alone, then you must realize that what you are you can not see in a mirror, and the self that you see in a mirror is but a dim reflection of your true reality. You do not see your ego in the mirror. You do not see your subconscious in the mirror. You do not see your inner self in the mirror. These are but terms. They are symbols to express the inner part of you that you cannot see nor touch. Within you, within the selves that you know, is the prime identity, the whole inner self.

ESP CLASS SESSION, JANUARY 14, 1969
TUESDAY

You do not have the kind of brandy that I drink, nor indeed could you come close to approximating the quality.

(There was a class discussion of the adjustment to be made going from death on the physical plane to "spirit" plane.)

That is frightening, but it goes to show you that even I have things to learn... That the shock of birth is far greater than the shock of death. For when you are born again, then you must completely readjust and learn to operate in a strange and alien environment. When you die, there are no such strong adjustments. Circumstances vary, but if you are lucky—and I hope you will be lucky—then your intellectual faculties will continue to operate. Attending this class they certainly should. And so there is instead triumph, for you say, "I am dead, and still I am I" You will dance a merry dance!

But when you are born again into a tiny and helpless organism and when your intellect may still be operating strongly, then there is a shock, for you cannot do what you want to do. You take it for granted that you can express yourself, and you cannot. That is a shock. Some individuals will retain strong memories of their past lives, and others will not. It is easier, you see, if you do not remember.

It does you no good as an infant to recall your success of a life past in your terms, for then you feel twice as helpless. Death is indeed triumphant. Our friend Ruburt feels triumph in this life to have lived as many years as he has, and to find himself strong and hearty—for he feared that adulthood would destroy him. And *(to Sue)* that is also your own fear.

Then how much more triumphant you will feel, when you realize you have lived and died many times and managed to survive, as indeed I have managed to survive.

I came through this evening to let you know that I like your home *(to Rachel, where the class session was being held)*.

(Class discussed whether Seth had been here before.)

Now, I have not been so social here before, and if you are not careful I shall see that you return to your dead bonfire. Not that you have not been there in your dreams, and there will be other times in classes when we will be there, and you will decide to leave the group and take the journey that will take you there. And then you will feel triumph. Now this wine is more to my liking.

Now *(to Theodore)*, you will have a session when the time is ripe. I am demanding more of you because you are working. You must, you see, develop in your own way and I do not want to color developments. I am not unaware of your activities, nor of yours *(to Vera)*, but it is tempting for me to take the easy way out. It is, indeed.

(There was discussion with Maureen as to Seth's reality.)

When *(to Maureen)* I truly believe that you exist, then I will expect you to believe that I exist. Until then, keep your own opinion. I find it enjoyable and somewhat amusing, but I always respect the workings of honest skepticism and intellectual critical analysis. It is good and healthy.

In my own book, for an intellectual exercise—and simply for that, since I do believe that all of you do exist—I am going to deal in one chapter with the difficulties of proving—from my vantage point—that three-dimensional reality does exist and is inhabited by creatures—thinking creatures.

For how do I know as I sit here that you are not the products of my imagination? I am indeed an imaginative gentleman, and have been for centuries. And how do I know that I do not simply want to teach and so imagine a roomful of pupils?

In the intellectual development of the idea I shall, of course, decide that you exist. Though to do so I must follow you in your pursuits through the days. For how do I know that you exist if I do not see you? Otherwise, you take it for granted, you see, that your physical bodies are quite obvious. They may be to you but to me they are highly hallucinary.

You think that the bodies that you have are permanent, but it is highly difficult for me to see the specific bodies that you now occupy, since I see you in all your reincarnational involvements and some of them have been highly involved indeed!

You *(to Theodore)* see a composite personality. In your terms, I see a composite personality. In my terms, I see you. It is you who break down your identity into various selves.

You *(to Sue)* will survive adulthood—many adulthoods. You have survived many.

You *(Daniel)* also will survive. Unfortunately you will have to work and use your mind. You like to use your mind. However, do not use it as a plaything but as a tool—a fine one.

Welcome *(to Florence, just arrived from her class)* to our class on abnormal psychology.

Soon, you see, you will all be able to read the Seth material. You all have good minds. You are not used to using them. You set up barriers and gates and limitations, and the material demands your high intellectual focus. I want you to use your intuitions, but I also want you to use your intellects. Some of you still have to learn to use them and how to give them freedom. I spoon-fed you. And I added a bit of sugar here and there. But if you continue here in classes, more and more you will have to give. You will have to give your high intellectual purpose and learn to use your minds as you never used them before. I am a tricky old character.

([Rachel:] "And a lovable one.")

I am glad that you find me lovable. But I will trick you into using your minds. You must use all of your abilities. You will need them. And if you do well, you see, you can solve problems now. And if you are good you can skip a class, which means skip a reincarnation. The more problems you solve now, the fewer you will have to solve later.

SESSION 1/14/1969

That does not mean that you will not have new challenges in other dimensions, for so you will. Think of the challenges that I have, for I must awaken you, and lead you onward and shake you up.

Now, our friends *(Rachel's neighbors)* are not used to me. They will not automatically think that Ruburt is out of his head tonight. And if they hear my voice they will simply think that our friend is simply talking in his sleep. So you see I feel I have some freedom. Of course, we may not be invited here again.

([Rachel:] "You are always welcome, night or day.")

You are always welcome to Seth's house. Ruburt does not take kindly to that remark.

Now *(to Florence)*, I had contemplated being—if you will excuse the expression—deathly quiet after your arrival. I also like a good joke.

However, I knew that if you knew I had spoken earlier you would feel rejection, and I do not want you to feel rejection—except when I want you to feel rejection!

I want all of you to learn enough and think enough so that you will be able to read my material on your own—word by word—and understand what I am trying to say without the sugar coating and the frosting, though frosting is good.

I have indeed been here before, but then I have been in all the residences of our students. To show you that I have utmost concern for your neighbors I will keep my voice low. In any case, I will give you all a break, and if ever you crash into pieces I will pick you up. I may not be able to put them together again but I will pick them up. Now relax. You have nothing to fear but me. Awaken yourselves of humor—it is lost in the bulrushes *(after a pun from Florence).*

([Florence:] *"I'm sorry, Seth, I was thinking that the last time I spoke to you I was in an airplane bouncing all over Utica. All I thought of was breaking into pieces."*

([Rachel:] *"I have the feeling that the other personality is very close by. There are times that it seems to be pulling you in. Your voice is a little high for Seth."*

(Here followed a discussion of Jane's masculine actions and gruff voice when Seth comes through.)

I am not gruff. I do not bark.

([Rachel:] *"I mean <u>as</u> masculine. There is no gender to him. Now where do I go from here?"*)

... is not sugar coated. But in our sessions in class I have spoken—if you will forgive me on a simple level. Leading you, I hope, sweetly and gently up the path that I want you to follow, and broadening your ideas so that you will be able to read the regular Seth material and follow it.

([Theodore:] *"Now is that the primrose path?"*)

The primrose path has many thorns and you are beginning to walk it. All of you, you see, with two exceptions—these two *(Sue and Daniel)*—you have been so caught in organizational realities and daily practicalities that you have leashed your intellects. It is not that you do not have good intellects. It is that you have made a bargain with yourselves. And the bargain is, that you will not use your intellects fully so that you can manipulate more comfortably in your own environment. Now, I hope to show you that you <u>can</u> use your intellects fully and still operate more effectively in your environment.

You must also use your intuitions. The intuitions know first, but there is no reason why your intellects cannot follow. None of you in this room use 50% of your intellect and there is no reason why you cannot use it. None of you use 50% of your intuitional abilities, and there is no reason why you cannot use the abilities.

Our friend here, our Lady from Florence, shines simply because she uses 20% more of her intellect. But in contrast to what you could use, this is nothing. And you *(Florence)* must not compare yourself to others, but compare yourself to your own potential. Now, the others in this room use perhaps 20% of their intuitional abilities and you have been using perhaps 10%. So you have a balance to make up on that score. These dimensions and these realities you can understand. You can experience them for yourself to some degree if you but try.

Now these two *(Sue and Daniel's)*—I'm getting to them at a fairly young age in this life. This one *(Sue)* has abilities from past lives to deal with and to use—and a greater responsibility to use them. This one *(Daniel)* has the idea that he can skim on through. This is no fun life. It is a work life for you and it is a time for you to produce and develop, and to use your abilities on your own behalf and for others. There is every reason in the world why using your abilities in such a manner should be fun.

It should be a time of high adventure, but not a time of laziness—and not a time of skimming through.

You must remember when I speak to you and see you, that I do not see you at the ages that you are. In this life some of you are older and some of you are young, but as entities it may be the other way around. Some of you are very young entities and some of you are old. I would like to say that I am a junior entity—a young sprite. However, this is not the case. And I am pleased that it is not.

You wonder what I see when I look at you. I have an impression of the physical bodies which you now inhabit. But I also see, in your terms, your future and your past and the probabilities of your development, and the abilities that you have and must use.

([Rachel:] "How do we have the power to determine the future if past, present and future are all one?")

This is in your terms. To make an idea clear I must often resort to ideas of time that are current with you. You change constantly. Reaction is simultaneous, and yet you do have control. And in your own terms, I must often use past, present and future. Now when you read the material and all of it—you will find that your questions are well answered, for there is no question that you have that I have not anticipated. This is my job. You *(Rachel)* have the capacity if you use it—and the ability. I will stretch your IQ.

Ruburt will do the pulling. The abilities are there in each of you and you will use them. Before I am done with you, you will use your abilities. And *(to Florence)* you will use yours.

I wish you all good evening. Our friend over here *(Sally)*, however, was quite correct. I am now momentarily in that circle, and you know it well. And if you do not fight me, as is your privilege, then you can look across the circle and see my face, for I lift my head.

(There was class conversation about the "circle" after which Rachel spoke of the possibility of not coming to classes anymore.)

You are at all our classes. You brought yourselves together.

([Student:] "Were we brought together or are we here of our own free will?")

You brought yourselves together for a reason.

(Class discussion.

(Rachel:] "Why don't we say good-night?")

I bid you all good evening, but I will visit some of you this evening whether or not you will remember.

([Vera:] "Help us to remember. "

(Goodnights around and Theodore added, "Amen.")

You *(to Theodore)* had better watch it over there!

JANUARY 14, 1969, TUESDAY
CONVERSATION BETWEEN RACHEL AND RUBURT

(Ruburt:) "Rachel, if you stay in that circle it is false

security."

([Rachel:] *"I can't leave until I can see where I am going."*)

(Ruburt:) "There will be light. There will be light and somebody else... I think me."

([Rachel:] *"I'd say that way... "*)

(Ruburt:) "I just know it's false security to stay in the group."

([Rachel:] *"I know this."*)

(Ruburt:) "Because you have to go beyond that group at that time. Besides, there are two people in that group who are not really friendly. While they are here in this room now, frankly, they were not friendly at that time. I was one who was friendly at that time. It is only because I was there and you were there at that time, that you can now realize this. This is apparently some kind of neurosis that you picked up that you can get over now ... and only that you progressed so far in the end that you can. You have the opportunity to make adjustments and to leave the group when the night comes. You have the same sort of thing that Jane had, but Jane is getting over it egotistically in this life. Although Jane's ... was so strong she had to egotistically become more permissive. The sense of resistance has to do with the neurosis picked up in that time.

"<u>In that time</u>, you did not leave the group and you should have. Now you have the opportunity to go back and leave the group. It is as if in your terms, you see, you could go back to a period of this life where you should have acted in a different way and didn't. Well you have the opportunity now to go back into that existence and make it different in the present. Because you can change—now this is in our physical terms—you can change what we would think of as the past through actions in our present. Do you understand me?

"The past in our terms doesn't cause present behavior, because you can go back now into that past and change it in our present. You will have the opportunity to do it because of your intuitive understanding, and this is something that most people haven't developed enough to do. Now actually that circle and those people are as real as this room seems to the rest of you. Right now this room doesn't seem very real to me. Now you can if you want to—and without any kind of coercion—look up and see Seth's face. And in the face you'll find confidence to leave the group at that time. The confidence you find then will serve you now and help you in the daily life that you think you are leading now."

([Rachel:] "Who are the unfriendly ones?")

(Ruburt:) "Starting with yourself, counting yourself, the third person down to your left at that time was in conflict with you. The fourth person beyond them was also in conflict with you and you were frightened of them. And because of them you stayed in the group, lacking confidence to go ahead."

([Rachel:] "I think I was one of the unfriendly ones.")

(Ruburt:) "Wait a minute. Answer me, will you? Over a knoll... I feel a rise there."

([Rachel:] "Yes... a wheat field.")

(Ruburt:) "Okay. I don't want to give you any suggestions, so you'll have to answer me honestly. Do you sense anybody beyond that?"

([Rachel:] "No.")

(Ruburt.) "I sense somebody beyond that *(wheat field)* coming from the village that we talked about earlier; and I sense that you do not want to know that they are there."

([Sue:] "I'm the one across the field. "

([Rachel:] "This is it, Jane. I'm rejecting... I'm not getting to see faces, but I can see Seth.")

(Ruburt:) "You're all right then."

([Rachel:] "Jane, let's just forget it...")

(Ruburt:) "It's too late... "

([Theodore:] "Does she have to go by the two unfriendly figures to leave and reach the light?")

(Ruburt:) "No. There's only one figure out in the wheat field that she doesn't want to face."

(Conversation back and forth between Rachel, Ruburt and others about leaving and not leaving past group and present group.

(Continuing chatter about going from present to past—changing past and its affect upon the present.

(Seth:) Now cheer up!

([Rachel:] "Here comes my... He's going to help me.")

(Seth:) First of all you will not leave this group because you do not want to. You will work out your problems in the last group, and I will help you do so if you want me to.

([Rachel:] "You know I do. ")

(Seth:) I have a strong arm when it is mine. There are many probabilities and there is no problem.

([Rachel:] "They're of our own making, Seth.")

(Seth:) You quote me. If you remember that you have no problem, then that is the answer. You will not leave this group. If you want to, you will leave the other group—and with confidence. In one probability you have already done so.

(One week later, in class of January 21, Sue told of a recurring dream which she had for some years—a dream in which she had stood in a field of wheat or cornfield was afire and she feared for the safety of the village.)

ESP CLASS SESSION, JANUARY 21, 1969
TUESDAY

(Discussion about predestination led by Rose to say that Seth would make a good Presbyterian.)

I was not a good Presbyterian. I am a good Sethite, as Ruburt would say.

(There followed a discussion about the place of protest and violence in the world today—this violence as a means to correct injustice and to get people to accept all other people and their "thing" without prejudice or the judgment of someone else's values. Sue and Ned of the younger generation were proponents of "pro " and others were either "con" or neutral

or philosophical.)

You cannot kill. As long as you can extinguish a human consciousness forever, then murder and killing are crimes. And you must deal with them. As long as you believe in the reality of violence, then violence is a crime, and you reap its fruits. There will never be a justification for killing or violence.

Since there is no death, in your terms, there is no murder. We will have some long sessions dealing with this matter, but I tell you all now—no good will come of violence. The gains that seem to be won will end in the violence of those who bring them about. The violence will be reborn in them. It will be part of their reality, and others will turn against them. This applies to any people at any time.

If there is one message I would give to you all, it is that there is no justification for killing—there is no justification for hatred—there is no justification for violence. It may occur, but those who indulge in violence are themselves changed, and the purity of their purpose adulterated. They are no longer the selves that they were.

In the past, with few exceptions, attempts have been made to change the external situation. I have told you that if you look around you and do not like the world that you see, then it is yourselves individually and en masse that you must change. For this is the only way that change will be effected. And if your generation or any generation would ever effect a change—this is the only way change will be effected.

What I am telling you has been told throughout the centuries and the people have not listened. It is up to you now *(Sue and Ned)* whether or not you listen. It is wrong to curse a flower, and it is wrong to curse any man. And it is wrong <u>not</u> to hold any man in honor and it is wrong to ridicule any man. You honor yourselves. You see within yourselves the spirit of eternal vitality, and you honor it and you treat yourselves in that manner as gods. If you do not do this, then you destroy all that you touch. And you honor each other individual also, because in him is the spark of eternal vitality.

When you curse another you curse yourselves and the curse comes back to you. When you are violent for any cause, the violence returns. For that which you send out and that which you give you also receive. There is no other way. There has never been any other way. The laws are old and ancient.

I speak here because yours is the opportunity and yours is the time. Do not fall into the old ways that will lead you precisely into the world that you fear.

When every young man refuses to go to war you will have peace. As long as twenty men insist on fighting a war you will not have peace. As long as you fight for gain and greed you will not have peace. As long as one person commits violence for the sake of peace you will have war. Unfortunately, in the condition in which your world finds itself, it is extremely difficult to imagine that all the young men in all of the countries at the same time will refuse to go to war. And so you must work out the violence that violence has wrought.

Not in your physical time, but within the next hundred years, that time may come... *(phrase omitted)*... but when it comes, and if it comes soon it will come as a miracle. For it will come when every man realizes that killing is wrong, and when every young man in every country refuses to go to war, and when he refuses to curse any man or any flower. You do not defend any idea with violence. With violence you kill an idea.

Defend any psychic energy that you have now. This energy, en masse, could change the world in the twinkling of an eye if it were directed constructively.

(More discussion here.)

You cannot pay lip service to peace while you are violent.

ESP CLASS SESSION, FEBRUARY 4, 1969 TUESDAY

What Ruburt—someone had better take this down, or my friend will have nervous conniptions.

Now, what my friend Ruburt does not understand is very simple, people. For when my friend Ruburt looks at a person he sees a mind and he automatically grades it... A, B, C, D, E, F and if you fail the grade he washes his hands of you. His ego washes his hands. He is too intuitive, however, and, indeed, too good. So the inner self does not wash its hands, but his ego does not realize this most of the time. It does not want to play.

Children play and believe it or not the gods play, and they have a merry game. And so when I speak to you, I speak to you as people and as individuals.

I have lived many lives and have had high intellects and I have had low intellects. I have been intellectually stupid and I have been intellectually brilliant. And I have been intuitively brilliant and I have been emotionally dumb.

And I know that truth speaks to more than intellect, and there is a higher truth than intellectual truth, though intellectual truth is important and it can lead you in the right direction. But when I speak to you I speak to a part of you that the intellect does not know, and intellect can learn from that part of you to which I speak. In many cases intellectual truth follows intuitive truth. You know intuitively. Sometimes you must wait years for your intellect to catch up with what you know. And sometimes you must wait centuries.

Now I bid you welcome, I do not mean to put my good friend here too much on the griddle. I did it... I did it. You should use the intellect you have and the intuition that you have, but I sneak through the cracks. Where there are no doors I push through little cracks in your armor and in your wall. And through those cracks you find your own escape and your own freedom and your own ways to truth.

Knowledge does not exist without consciousness. There is no ideal knowledge that can be to given you that exists independently of consciousness. Consciousness knows. There is not an inert ideal thing called knowledge that you can drink up. I am a consciousness, and what you should know I try to tell you, and I try to teach you. But there are no records, despite any of your readings. There are no records, no bodies of knowledge that exist independently of consciousness. There are no records in the sky to be read. There are personalities who have knowledge that you do not yet realize you know. And they can tell you what they know to the best of their ability, as I do. And you learn in your own way, and you don't learn in your own way.

I will have an all night session whenever you are ready. And I can wear you all out. And I am as busy… and far busier than any of you are. Now, I know you individually and I am making no exceptions, and you know that I know you, each of you. We have a few star pupils. They are working very hard. And I congratulate them.

It seems that our Lady from Florence is not looking inward. It seems that she is not experimenting, it seems that she does not know in some large manner why she is here. Of all of you, she has had the fewest inner experiences, so it would seem, yet she is forbidding her own purposes by being here. And a portion of her personality knows what she is learning. And she knows that I have a spot in my invisible heart for her. And she fulfills a purpose in this class, and in this group, that is highly important, at the same time she is indeed fulfilling inner possibilities and opening roads.

(To Ned:) My nose, young man, is not a moving picture machine. You may look at it to your heart's content.

(To Rachel, Sally and Theodore:) Now, you also fulfill a purpose in the group, and still in coming to the group you also pursue your own purposes. And this is good. I know you are not about to leave the group. Not this group. Not unless my friend builds a fireplace. I promised you a session and you will have it and within the time limit. I make him work hard because he has the ability and is working. You particularly. *(To Theodore?)*

I will not give you easy answers, for they will not serve you. I will give you the opportunity to ask the correct questions, for in the past you have not known enough to know what they are. I will not lead those who would follow me blindly. And all of you take that to heart. For in following blindly you learn nothing. I demand that you work. In your own way, and according to your own abilities. But that you use you own individual abilities, and learn how to handle them. And you will. And learn what they are, and you will. And work out the relationship that exists in your immediate families. And both of you will. And learn the significance—the meaning behind the fact that your daughter and your sister are approximately the same age, and you will. They choose that relationship.

Now, there is no reason why truth should not be joyful, there is no reason why truth cannot play tricks, even with noses. And note to our friend, Ruburt—there is no reason why truth must necessarily be given in high intellectual tones. Now, I have given material in our own session that is highly legitimate and valid, and it will be used and used well by people who can understand it intellectually. And I have given material that is highly intuitional that will be understood and used by people who know how to use their intuitions. Truth does not follow a single line.

The sign of the younger generation. And to show that though I have no visible heart I am young at heart. I give you then indeed that sign *(V)*.

You *(to Rose)* are a young entity. Don't speak to me of youth and age. You are a very young entity and frisky!

And do not worry that your friend Ruburt will overdo. Do not worry that he be led on, with questions, so that I speak. I look out for him. But I appreciate your concern. He is stronger than he looks. And so am I.

David and Goliath *(refering to Daniel.*
([Daniel:] "Will I win?")

You will win whatever you want to win.

Now, I have been a woman in several reincarnations. And *[to Brad]* so have you. Many of the women here have been men in several reincarnations. You need both. You must be a mother and a father. You must have reincarnations in which you are a mother and a father. You must be both male and female. And had I not been both male and female, I would not be able to speak to you and you and you. For I would be imprisoned within the barriers of sexual perception. And you may change to your heart's content. It is good for you.

Now, I am giving my friend a lesson.... My friend

Ruburt.... In how to deliver the material. And he will know what I mean. You will not find secrets in the grasses, only weeds.

Intellectually you will understand the material, if you read it. I did not mean, earlier, to give the impression that I was poking fun at our friend's intellect, only that you can at times prevent him from reaching out to others as he should. I need and needed an intellect through which I could work so that our basic principles could be understood by those who were intellectually inclined. And so that the scientist and mathematicians, the religious men, the philosophers, could find no fault with our reasoning. Through Ruburt's books we can reach and help many individuals. But they will not be reached as I'm reaching those of you in this room.... Recording or no. Our friend Ruburt himself has not understood the meaning of our classes sufficiently. Nor the energy that exists here and that will reach beyond the confines of this room. Our friend over here *(Theodore)* has Ruburt's back. It is not a barrier to him.

I will not keep you until breakfast. When I am silent or have a long pause, it is not because I do not know what I want to say next. It is because I am speaking to you silently. And even when I speak silently, I speak with a loud and unmistakable voice.

The one thing that I want you to understand and that I try to tell is that information—truth—can only be given to you through the medium of human consciousness. Consciousness means personality.

When I am jovial and when you know me as I am, realize that I have been what I am for a long time—with alterations and changes and developments. And that as you sit here before me, you are far more than you know. And if it seems to you that I have said this on endless other occasions, indeed I have. When I say it and repeat it, I say it and repeat it for a reason. It is so that you will know that vitality is joyful, and that personality has eternal validity and that changes continue. And that as you challenge me, so shall you be challenged.

And now I shall leave you on tippy-toe. Vitality such as this knows no barriers, no deaths, and no endings. Only beginnings, and beginnings are joyful. Creativity is ever new. Now I bid you a fond good evening—and rejoice!

ESP CLASS SESSION, FEBRUARY 25, 1969 TUESDAY

(The first two paragraphs were for Sue and Ned Watkins. [They had just been married:])

.... your unity. And to feel your unity with All That Is—and know you are a part of it. You should have known that you could not escape my ceremony—and my ceremony is a ceremony of the skies and trees—and even of the grass. My ceremony is a ceremony that does not need ceremony —for it speaks through all seasons and it rises and it speaks through you. And as you sit here now so you have existed many times. And the ceremony is not new. Autumns and springs are not new. You sit here with new youth and new vitality—new, but ancient—for there is no newness that does not have an ancient heritage. You will walk down many alleyways and many front avenues, and so you have and so you will again, but in this life you will walk them together, as you knew you would. And you knew you would meet here and that I would speak to you here, and there is no beauty that you imagine that is not possible. The dreams that you have will come to pass but beware of the fears—for fears also come to pass—rip them out. The joys must be forever new—for they are new with an ancient heritage.

You must look into the face of vulnerability to find joy. You cannot find a joy unless you accept vulnerability. Even the gods know vulnerability—and that is why they live. And because I have known vulnerability, I am still alive. I give you then all the peace and joy that you can hold. But you cannot hold peace and joy like a stone in your hand. For it goes through you and out into others.

You need know—you need know nothing—you need know nothing in intellectual terms. You know all behind words, and in parts of you that are beyond speech. You do not need words. You do not need my words—but I speak them. I speak the words so you will realize you do not need them. And looking at you now, it is not that I see through you—it is that I see the yous that you do not realize you are. So lo—your joy and peace—and let it be with you in the old ways of these days, realizing that these days are always—and yet that there are more days than these, and other times and other places. And so peace and joy be with you in all days.

Now I bless you, but the blessings must come from yourselves. The real blessings must come from yourselves. You must realize that you are one with All That Is, and within you is the only one who can give blessings, and you must be willing to accept the blessing that only you can give, and the joy that only you can give to yourselves and to one another.

There should never be a word in any language that means repentance. There should only be a word that means, "I bless," for when you bless you do not need to repent. And when you accept a blessing, you do not need to repent. For when you realize how to accept a blessing, there is nothing to repent. Love of All That Is requires simply that you become open as air, for when you are open as air then the joy of All That Is flows through you indiscriminately, and there is nothing to repent. You only need repentance when you do not know joy. For within joy and within All That Is there is only glory that is only consciousness and song. There is only blessedness.

When you berate yourself for your sins, then you do not realize what joy is. And All That Is is consciousness and joy. Do you berate a flower that has one crooked stem? So in yourselves, know spontaneity. And in spontaneity you will find joy.

Spontaneity has its own discipline. You do not need to enforce discipline upon it. You need not enforce discipline upon it. Pretend that the bony tissue of your skulls does not exist. And let the energy of All That Is flow through you as indiscriminately as clouds through the skies. Do not say, "I will accept this and I will deny this." The knowledge that is within yourselves knows. You do not have to fear the spontaneous. You do not need to fear that if you allow yourselves freedom you will travel into evil ways. Conscious restraints can lead you into avenues of denial. But the inner selves, knowing their position within All That Is, do not fear denial. What appears to you as evil is a result of your own ignorance. There is purpose in all things. In your spontaneity then, never forget the sacred uniqueness of a shadow upon a road, the shape of a leaf, the stain upon a coffee cup—in these simple things find a hint of your own uniqueness and travel beyond them—and ignore conscious restraint that would bind you. Let the inner intuitive sense speak for it is the inner voice, and the magic that unites you has no need of conscious words.

(Seth discusses the "two groups" regarding Rachel's question.)

Now—there are also emotional equations—and you are involved in an emotional equation. There is no situation from which you must escape in your inner group. There is a change that you have set for yourself and you have set up your own equation—and those in the class who are in both groups have their own equations—and in solving the emotional equations, you end up with spiritual clues. There is nothing from which you have to escape.

There are truths which you are trying to approach. There is nothing from which you have to hide. There are truths which you are trying to discover. The campfire is highly symbolic, and it has different meanings for all of you who experience it. This does not mean that the campfire is not real. It is very real. It has a reality as legitimate as this room—but not the same kind of reality. The qualities of the equation have highly subjective meanings, and they need not be the same meanings to each of you who are involved with them. And I am in both circles. So I am a common denominator. And I am a friendly common denominator. And when you hear me speak, it is not only my vitality that you hear, but it is also your own vitality—for I am also a part of All That Is—and if I am ancient and new, so are you ancient and new. And there are miracles in this room, and miracles in each and every room which you must learn to perceive. There are joys and vitalities within you which you do not perceive, that you must learn not to understand intellectually but to <u>feel</u>. And you think because I speak to you when you are here that I belong here. But I am a part of no particular room and no particular time and no particular place. And you are a part of no particular room and no particular time and no particular place. Now to others that you do not perceive, you are as magical, you are as nebulous as a shadow falling upon a floor in midafternoon. They do not perceive you. And as they may not see your magic and your consciousness, so there are other magic shadows and other realities that you think beneath you that you do not perceive. But

All That Is is aware of each shadow. And knows that each shadow... *(break because of end of tape.)*

... realities that they know. And my reality transcends this room. Then so does your reality transcend this room. And if Ruburt has access to <u>my</u> reality and if my reality sings through him...then my vitality is but a hint of All That Is—and that tiny and insignificant echo of the reality of all that exists.

And the inner self that controls your breathing does not need you to consciously discipline it. And if you try to consciously discipline it then, indeed you can tamper with its beautiful, spontaneous order.

(As Rachel departed, she mentioned that the old saying that, "one can only be sure of two things—death and taxes," is no longer true. To which Seth added.) You can be sure of life—and I bid you good evening.

(Jane pointed out to Sally that she was playing it too safe, that she should take some risks. She should explore more, she continued, and that there was nothing to be frightened of. Jane said Florence could attempt "a tiny look within" and find out there's nothing to be frightened of there either, and that she could give her intuitions free reign. That she and Daniel can look each other in the eyes as people. And that, "at least in this room you can allow yourself this freedom.")

And then when you hear my voice, you hear your own. And when you feel my presence, you feel your own presence. And there is no need to hide from either. I want you to feel my words imprinted where you cannot take notes safely in a notebook. And I want you to question, but honest questions—not questions that are cover-ups for other questions. And when you have real questions, as you know, I answer them. And when they are not honest questions, I do not answer them. And I do not give you credit for easy answers. I do not give you multiple choices—I want essays. But my essays I want delivered from the inner portion of yourself—that is composed of intuition and intellect. And look up Lady of Florence—I will not let you settle for easy answers. And I will not let you settle for easy questions. And I will not give you easy answers. And I will not give you wonders. I will make you produce your own wonders. And you would not want it otherwise. And that is why we understand each other so well. You have known many who have offered you easy answers and answered your easy questions. But you do not like them as well as you like me.

[Break:]

I will now bid you a fond good evening—and I meant to meet my eyes, not to be downcast. And you are, indeed, off to the right, inner portions of your personality this evening—attending two classes—and you do not have to pay $3 for the other class *(to Theodore)*.

I did not come through purposely lately because I do not want you to take it for granted that I will speak at each class. You do not work as hard. Now if Ruburt's eyesight is poor, there is nothing wrong with mine. And when I speak at class, as I have told you often, I have a purpose. And <u>my purpose</u> is to remind you that the vitality and meaning of existence is within you. And that the energy within this room is available to you. And when I come pussyfooting into this room, it is also to remind you that there is peace within you—expect it and look for it—it is there. And peace is not a dead thing. Peace rings with the vitality of the universe. And it sings throughout your blood and it is a part of All That Is. Then relax and accept it—and remember, I have lived many physical lives as you are living physical lives now. And I have survived in good and hearty fashion—and so will you. And with your intellect and with your reason, and even I, as both male and female, have been married without ceremony and with ceremony and the true marriage has nothing to do with ceremony of that kind. The true meeting is a spiritual meeting and can be expressed in many ways...and a flower exists in a field whether a minister blesses it or not—for it is a part of All That Is and, therefore within it, it carries its own blessing and its own meaning.

And before our Ruburt worries too much about his neighbors, I wish you all a fond good evening. And when you sleep, your vitality will still ring as my voice rings, though you may not hear the peal.

ESP CLASS SESSION, APRIL [1?], 1969
(SPECIFIC DATE UNKNOWN)

(M.D. believes the class was April 1, 1969 based on two subjects mentioned in the class: Easter was on April 6 and the anniversary of Martin Luther King's assassination

was April 4.)

This one here has come some long way and rides herself rather hard, because I am behind her with the whip. I would not use it. Now, since I am also going to be an author you must look upon me with some awe. Ruburt may not want me to get into the act. I should not joke about him for he is indeed as he said earlier, delighted. It is not often that we have this one here with us.

Now, I would clear up one or two small points. First of all, I have been about to hear some of your excellent dissertations on my behalf. Secondly, I was also about when one member *(Florence)* of this class and another woman were working on my book. The other woman [*was*] your daughter, of course, I get about. You are all in a fine mood now and when I tell you you are awake, you are awake. There is no one that can wake you up like I can and in more ways than one. Ruburt will be on to me. He has a session tomorrow evening and he had a session last night, but he does not bother me over much.

I am here most seriously because I am pleased with your interest in the material and because book 1 is here now and completed. The interest and the effort mean much to you and will work for your own benefit, beside the fact of course, that you will have in your possession an excellent manuscript. I am sorry that I do not move tables as well as AA, but were I interested in moving tables, I can assure that this one would fly through the window and end out in the middle of Water Street! I am more interested in other projectiles and other movement, thoughts that fly through your minds rather than tables that leap about the floor. These have far more reality and far more resources.

You are doing well as a lecturer of note. See that you do not make any errors or I will tap you on the shoulder. It has been a very pleasant visit.

It was difficult for me to remain so quiet all evening long, but since I could not send you a postcard of thanks, I thought I would thank you personally. Ruburt enjoyed your sparkling brew so, and so now I also to some slight extent can enjoy it. Before this brings to your mind hilarious images of tipsy spirits, if you will excuse the pun, I will leave you to the rest and quiet in which I found you, perhaps.

Some evening you may dance the hula through my aura. I will make it skip about the room. As long as you do your work and study, I am jovial. There is always a purpose behind what I say and behind what I do.

([Florence:]) "When I think of the millions and millions of lives that have been sacrificed in the name of Christ, in the name of God, the Jewish slaughtered back in the middle centuries with the—in the Crusades—in the name of Christ. You said the spirit of Christ had entered every person, and yet mankind does not reflect this. Watching the turmoil on television today, just one spark could have set off an explosion that would rock this country, just one Negro had been pushed around too much by a white policeman. Seth said before that there is not just one Christ, not just one person that did all the things that Christ did, but many people."

(Group discussed the concept of Christ.)

Do you think that the Son of God could be contained in one frame? Now, you have been given the free will because the spirit of Christ is within you, this does not mean that you do not have free will. The spirit of Christ gives you the life to do with it what you choose. Within you there are blueprints. You know what you are to achieve, as individuals and as people, as a race, as a species. You have free will, you can choose to ignore the blueprints. You can choose to ignore the blueprints for some time. You are learning that you are responsible. When you learn how to handle responsibilities, you will have a hand in very important matters.

Now, you have made physical reality something different than was intended. You did this through using your own free will, your egos have become overdeveloped, overly specialized. They are focused so strongly within physical reality and physical reality is far more painful than was originally intended. You are indeed in very strong respects within a dream. It is you who have made the dream too vivid. You were to work out problems and challenges, but you were always to be aware of your inner reality and of your true home. To a large extent you have lost contact with this. You have focused so strongly upon physical reality that it has become, indeed, reality. The only reality that any of you know.

When you kill a man, most of you believe that you have killed him forever. And murder, therefore, is a crime and must be dealt with as such because you have created it and you must deal with it. You have created the crime. Death does not exist in those terms. In the dawn of history, in the dawn before history began, man changed form. They knew they *(did not die)*.

Listening to your tape, I see that I did not make one point clear. And it is this, then. No god created the crime of murder, and no god created sorrow and pain. The hour is late, and my friend Ruburt did not want me to speak loudly for long. What I have said, however, should serve to remind you when you question that these things were created by yourselves as you forgot your true beginnings, and only when you remember your beginnings will these cease.

Now, I bid you good evening and welcome here. You have been given but glimpses of what I am trying to explain to you but what I will explain will make your own reality as you know it more meaningful and will give a logical and intuitive basis to it, which is lacking.

One small point here for my friend Ruburt, and that is that I did, indeed, enjoy the Saturday evening session. It was amusing to see such a good counterfeit image of myself *(Carla C.)*.

You all should definitely have a basic understanding of the material, for it is the material that will help you discover your own identities and which will make other realities meaningful to you as you are now. What I can tell you now is little, for you do not have the basic background that is required. Had you by now read the material I could be giving you further data. As it is, I cannot do so.

   I came this evening because we had a guest and also because you would know that I had not indeed deserted you. I am here whether or not I speak, you see, and often I inspire Ruburt, so that when he speaks himself, he speaks for me. For I am crafty in my ways. Now, I do indeed give you my heartiest regards and wishes, and were it not for Ruburt's wishes and the lateness of the hour and his concerns about the neighbors, I would continue. However, I also know that there have been parties going on in this room well past midnight. With music blaring from all the walls and no one said, "Turn off the music, for the neighbors will be worried." I do admit my voice, as it came through here, may not be as melodious. I am no disc jockey. Nevertheless, there is a point here that my friend Ruburt would do well to take to mind. I will speak to you again shortly. I could not let you leave, you see, with heavy hearts and disappointed faces. Far be it for me to blacken your day and send you away without a present! Not that I compare myself with any Easter time gift, you understand. However, I know that you look forward to my jolly comments.

   You had better all get on your toes and get to work or we will not have very many jolly comments. I do not come on tippy-toe like the white Easter bunny with a white floppy tail through the tulips! My material, you must admit, is rather heavy and can become ponderous at times, but you will understand yourselves far better and the world in which you live, and the tulips, if you study the material. And with that jolly little message, I will leave you all. I hope peacefully for this evening—I go reluctantly, but I do not leave quietly. I have come mainly to let you know that I am here.

The physical bodies that you have are real only within your perspective. You have formed these bodies with senses that react only within this perspective.

You are stuck with what you have created. I will have our friend here get out some of the old material because you must understand precisely how these physical constructions are made, and I have gone into them from several viewpoints. But because you do believe that you can murder a man, then murder does exist within your system, and you must deal with it.

Give me a moment. Your Dr. King is now precisely what he always was. The man who killed him believes he has killed a man, and ended consciousness forever and blotted out for eternity something that existed for a very brief time. And to believe that you have done such a thing is indeed pitiful. To bring yourself to do such a thing, when this is what you believe, is indeed pitiful. But your errors and your mistakes luckily enough are not real and do not affect reality. For Dr. King indeed exists.

ESP CLASS SESSION, APRIL 8, 1969
TUESDAY

It is time to bring the meeting to order because it *is*

time to take most of you to task. I am speaking to the regular members of this class. You are hiding from yourselves—you are not thinking deeply—you are not looking into yourselves, and you are making little effort to use your intuitional abilities or your intellectual abilities. And you *(to Brad)* are looking for others to tell you what to do.

Now, if you have learned anything in here, you must realize that when you tread a superficial web, you fall under. The inner strengths that are available to you, you are not using. Social discourse lately has been your profundity. You can indeed be more profound than that. This evening in class, you were not able to use your inner abilities. Now it is not often that I speak severely to you. But if I did not speak severely to you, then who would? You have seen, and you continue to see what can be done—and you have seen others come to class with no experience and little knowledge. You have seen our dweller in the hall here *(Theodore)* use his abilities—and he does not need to look for wonders because he is experiencing reality.

And our dear Lady of Florence: you have not yet put one tippy-toe in the clear waters of the inner self. You have not even danced about the shore. These inner realities represent your freedoms and your triumphs and your strengths—they represent the wonders that are within you—they cannot be given to you by another. No man's reality is the same, whether it be physical or spiritual reality. You close the door to your own heritage when you do not look inward.

You close the door to your own strength when you

look for it in another *(to Brad)*. If I solved your problems for you, there would be no need for you to use your own inner resources. There would be no need for you to look inward and recognize your own abilities. And it would indeed be a betrayal of you on my part to treat you in such a manner. You have had easy solutions offered you in the past and they were not solutions, they were threats. I tell you that you have within yourself the ability to solve your problems. You have within yourself the ability to stand up and make your way. You also have the responsibility to discover who and what you are. The answers to your problems lie within yourself and you can discover them—and in discovering them, you use your strength. To rely upon others will only encourage weakness. Therefore, I will not allow you, you see, to use me as a crutch. I will throw your crutches away—and give you a good hard push and make you stand up and face your problems alone. And that is the only way I can help you. And that is the only way you can ever be helped and you know it, and you know it well. And I mean it kindly.

Now you are _all_ getting it this evening, but it is long due—and it is for this reason that our friend Ruburt did not welcome me with open arms at your last class, for he knew what I was up to. It does you no good for me to come here and give you a symbolic pat on the back, and say, "My chickadees, fly away—you are doing well!"—not when you are _not_ doing well. You are _not_ fulfilling your responsibilities to yourselves simply by coming here once a week. You _are_ fulfilling your responsibilities when you go within yourselves every day. Is the journey, after all, <u>that</u> frightening? The fear is only what you have created yourself. You have made it and placed it before the door.

Now, you *(Florence)* have given your son a car—and why? Is it a vehicle that will carry him back to your heart—ask yourself such a question honestly and look for your answers. You can use your love of your son as a vehicle —and as a vehicle that will help you find yourself.

Now, if I did not know your potentials, then I would not bother you. If all of you did not have abilities that you were not using, I would leave you alone. For to needle you would be cruel and I am <u>not</u> cruel. But I needle you in a righteous cause, and each of you knows it well. The search upon which you have all embarked can only be begun from the center of your own reality. This is what you have to work with. And you have more to work with than you realize. Demand <u>more</u> of yourself- not less. Your *(to Rose)* information was quite legitimate *(this referred to a letter Rose received from England).*

(Seth was quite intense in his delivery of the preceding material—more so than usual.)

Now, to begin with, you must take the time. There is no doubt to whom I am speaking *(Vera)*. I welcome you formally *(to Jenny and Laurie)*. You *(Rose)* are doing well but you are still going very cautiously. You can have far more results even within the context within which you are working—if it were not for this overcaution. But you are making an effort, and where little effort is made, little results can be expected.

When *(to Florence)* there is a mathematical problem in which you are interested, you try to solve it. You do not solve it by standing in front of it with your arms crossed and closing your eyes and saying, "Surely the solution must be fearful." Now again, if our Lady from Florence did not have the ability to look inward, I would not try to force her to do so. But you do have the ability.

Now I would tell you, take one tippy-toe out of your physical time *(to Florence)*—only one tippytoe, and you will be surprised at the results. If you take the physical time, if you only take 15 minutes a day and make the effort to do so, this will automatically lead on your part to an initiation in the inner self. For the very fact of taking the time will represent a commitment which thus far you have not been willing to make. You had better open that door yourself—or someday I will huff, and I will puff, and I will blow the door down—and <u>then</u> there will be a mighty panic! And what have we here! And all it takes from you is the smallest whisper. You could at least speak through the keyhole. I will tell you, you will not find the answers you are seeking in any other way. There is no other way to find them. And again, you know this way.

Now, there is a tower of strength—but it is not outside yourself, but within yourself. And may I ask you *(Brad)* in all seriousness, dear friend, who—<u>who</u> do you think you are to refuse to use the strength which has been given to you. And why do you believe that the energy of the universe which flows through frog and tree—does not flow also through your own being—or to refuse to use this tremendous energy because you feel you are unworthy. Is a stone unworthy? For the sun falls upon the stone, and the stone does not say, "Lo and behold, I am a simple stone and not worthy for the sun to fall upon me." And a flower does not say, "Lo and behold, I am one small flower. In a million universes, who am I that I should grow and develop?" It uses its abilities <u>spontaneously</u> and with <u>joy</u>. Then also, use your own, and accept the energy and strength that is available to you. One flower cannot ask <u>another</u> flower for the sunshine—for the other flower cannot give it. But the sun is there and it shines upon all flowers. Therefore, do not look to another for help—for the help is there and available for you to use. Avail yourself of it.

Now, to prove to you that I am a good and hearty fellow and that I do not always wear a long disastrous face with a chin upon the floor, I will leave you and let you partake of your social discourse. And if you can be merry after this, then all the more power to you. And if you had more of a feeling of joy, you would look inward more easily and if you approached it as a child again, you would find some freedom.

Now, perhaps I do not use the correct approach with you *(Florence)* when I speak of responsibility, but you are responsibility oriented. But a flower does not feel the responsibility to bloom in the sun, it blooms because it is natural to bloom. And it is natural to look inward—it is only you who have set up these barriers and now find it so difficult to break them. And when you begin, I can

SESSION 4/8/1969

hear you now—"Why didn't I know earlier. Instead of hells, I find meadows—instead of darkness, I find light! Why did you not tell me?" Well, I am telling you now—and I will say I told you so.

(At this point Vera commented that Seth had not "lighted into her.")

I do not light into you. I have not the heart to light into you, because you are also giving him *(Theodore)* strength and you represent a foundation of which he is sure. Psychically you are giving very strongly of yourself in the entire family relationship, in an infinite life-giving way that is extremely important. You are a mother in a way that many mothers are not, and the psychic awareness within you and its vitality goes out like rays to give vitality to your children.

But *(still to Vera)* I do not want you to feel left out. What a heavenly smile indeed! I am glad I am in the company of saints! Now take your break.

(Florence said she remembered a dream from the preceding week.)

A <u>dream</u>! <u>I will give you a gold medal</u>! I will visit you in a dream and I will be nice and gentlemanly and you will remember.

(Class took its break and then Florence related her dream in which she found herself to be the neglected one.)

You are the flower that is telling itself not to grow. You can counter this—and to some extent your attendance in class does counter it. You can counter this by changing your attitude. Where is your courage? You are extremely courageous in the exterior environment. We take on racial problems—we deal with the weighty issues of our community. We tend to look boldly and courageously into the problems of our society—but lo and behold, what happens to our courage when we think of looking into ourselves. Now, you are not being intellectually honest by refusing to look into yourself. You are using your intellect instead as an excuse. You are saying, intellectually I will not operate in this particular area. You think you are saying, I am too intellectual to operate in this particular area—my intellect impedes my progress. Your <u>intellect</u> does not impede your progress, your <u>attitude</u> towards your intellect does. Your intellect can be used to examine your progress. It can be an aid and it can help you in your achievement. Your intellect is <u>not afraid</u> of the inner self. It will grow with you gladly and as a friend if you will allow it to do so. Pretend then that the inner self is another land—and that you are a tourist—and highly curious—that you are intellectually and intuitively curious—pretend that all this courage you use in your daily endeavors is an aid to help you find your way in this new and strange and wondrous environment. <u>Imagine</u> yourself using all the abilities, as you look inward, that you use daily in looking outward.

The problems exist in the inner realms—you can solve them there. You help indeed by trying to solve them in your community and in your society. But they will actually be solved in inner reality. Use all of your courage and your brain and solve the problems at their <u>source</u>.

Find out what the nature of inner reality is. You can then use inner reality as a secure basis from which you can look outward and see the world's problems more clearly and in better focus.

I will let our friend *(Ruburt)* rest—but I will stay in focus—and you had all better stay in focus!

(During class break Jane commented that Seth had a real purpose this night.)

I always indeed have a purpose! By all means now—*(to Brad)* give me a summary! I am always interested in how much you remember of what I say at least on a conscious level. Are you going to take your 15 minutes a day *(to Florence)*? Are you *(to Brad)* going to cease looking for answers from the outside? Are you going to try <u>seriously</u> to use your own strength?

([Brad:] "I have to.")

You do, indeed, and all of you do!

Now, I do not make a practice of being severe with young ladies with whom I am not well acquainted—therefore, I am letting you both off the hook. This does not mean, however, that you can expect such good treatment all the time. You *(Laurie)* will be here again and I will get to you.

You *(Jenny)* will need to find the stability to match your high intuition. You *(to Sally)* were not hanged in a past life—your crimes were not that severe.

Now I have said what I came here to say this evening. And you all know that there is fondness behind my severity. And you <u>all</u> know I would not huff and puff and blow your door in unless I gave proper warning—and I am giving proper warning! Now, there is joy in all this—and there is spontaneity—and you do not have to think in terms of walking into the inner self in a sack of ashes and crying repentance. If I had gold stars, I would paste one on his *(Theodore's)* forehead—but then he would be the one who would have to go to the bank and explain the strange star and not I.

The reason and the origin and the joy of your existence is within you all. And if you let it speak, then indeed it can speak within you in a voice as loud and joyous as any I dare use within the confines of this room. My voice is turned up to show you once again that vitality and your search is not sorrowful and is not for repentance, but is a joyful—and ambitious—and lively thing—and that the energy within you flies through your own being as the birds fly though the sky. And indeed, even as my voice reverberates against the ceiling, be thankful that it does not bounce and fall down and break into rocks upon the floor.

There is always a reason whether I whisper or whether I shout. Energy can be transformed into many patterns and used in many ways. And the energy that can indeed sweep through this smaller plane can be used for many purposes. And I hope it can be used to lead to your instruction because you can all use it!

(At this point class took a break.)

I am not tired out—my friend Ruburt is not tired out. But I am sorry that you are tired out. I would not tire you out for the world—it does not befit a good host.

(Class took another break and there was a discussion of sleepwalking.)

Now, since it is nearly midnight I will leave you—before I turn into a pumpkin! But to a very real extent, you are <u>all</u> sleepwalkers—for you are <u>far</u> more awake and far more alert in many of your sleep states than you are now. And use many of your abilities to much greater advantage then for there is a much higher state of wakefulness that you do not realize—and yet you know it well. There are states of perception with which you are intuitively aware but that escape you in the light of day.

And if you would work, and if you would look inward, and if you would explore the levels of your own reality and the levels of your own consciousness, then you would know what this state is—and you would remember it—and you would always have its reality as a guide.

Now our Dean has not experienced this yet. Our friend Ruburt <u>has</u>—and several of you have the ability to do so. And it would make your ordinary everyday intellect seem like an idiot child indeed—for you have no idea of the ability of your intellect as it really operates. Now I speak to you not idly—and these are not mere promises thrown about. These are realities that you can experience. These are a portion of <u>your own</u> as well as mine.

You <u>can</u> mount the steps of your own consciousness. Then <u>do so</u>. No one will boot you back down the stairs. Now I bid you all a fine good evening—and I give you what blessings I have to give.

I have enjoyed myself.

Tell him *(Ruburt) I* do not want him wearing any false eyelashes in our sessions—they do not fit my personality!

False eyelashes would not fit his personality any more than they would fit mine.

(Rose discussed reincarnation and stated her desire that the <u>door</u> not quite be closed for her "next one"—she wanted to be able to peek back and use some of her previous experiences.)

The door is <u>never</u> closed. It is <u>always</u> open. You only imagine that it is closed. No one closes the door but you. And no one makes you close the door—and no one can make you <u>open</u> the door <u>though I can certainly try</u>!!

JANE'S IMPRESSIONS: THEODORE MULDOON, APRIL 8, 1969

Something about the third man who could possibly be in control or something—definitely won't be. But I think this has to do with that other stuff so you should check it. I get, Theodore, that anything involving Syracuse would, with you directly up there I guess, be definitely more confining than down here no matter what it looked like ahead of time. And something about—anything involving Syracuse would involve you as a figurehead only—no matter what you have been told ahead of time. And that there are still expansions down here—and that at least one of them could emerge or appear more clearly within a fairly short time now, say ninety days. That its outlines for this would start to make sense and emerge, but that there would still be something else here. And that two things would actually emerge from what seems like one thing down here. Would look like one thing but two things would be involved, actually.

ESP CLASS SESSION, APRIL 22, 1969
TUESDAY

Now, emotions flow through you like storm clouds—or like blue skies—and you should be open to them and react to them—and let them pass. <u>You</u> are not your emotions. They flow through you. You feel them. And then they disappear. When you attempt to hold them back, you build them up like mountains—and you form tornadoes within yourselves.

I have told our Dean that spontaneity knows its own discipline. Your nervous system knows how to react. It reacts spontaneously when you allow it to do so. And the clouds flow through the thick skull easily. Now when you attempt to hold them back, it is then that they collect—and the electric charges grow—and the storm clouds grow.

You do not trust your inner selves sufficiently, nor the knowledge that you have within you.

Now I have been <u>drastically maligned</u> here this

evening! And so I come to show our new friend here that I am a jolly fellow. That, at least initially, was my intention.

However, with this talk of <u>discipline</u> and <u>spontaneity</u> my intention has somewhat changed. For I must tell you again, and I cannot tell you too often, that the inner self, acting spontaneously, automatically shows the discipline that you do not as yet understand. You are not your physical body. You are not your emotions. You have emotions as you have bacon for breakfast. You are not the bacon—and you are not your emotions. You have thoughts as you have eggs for breakfast. You are not the eggs and you are not your thoughts. You are as independent of your thoughts and your emotions as you are of the bacon and the eggs. You use the bacon and the eggs in your physical composition; and you use your emotions and your thoughts in your mental composition. Surely all of you consider yourselves somewhat superior to a piece of bacon, and you do not identify with it. Then, do not identify with your emotions or your thoughts. They flow <u>through</u> you. You attract them in the same way you go to the store to buy your bacon. But the bacon goes through your physical system and the thoughts of emotion, left alone, will pass through your psychic system. And you are independent of them. When you set up barriers and doors, then you enclose these thoughts within you—as if you stored up tons of bacon in your refrigerator and wonder why there was not enough room for anything else.

You have yet to learn to be free. You are not physical

matter; you are not your thoughts; you are not your emotions. You <u>have</u> emotions; you <u>have</u> thoughts; you <u>have</u> a physical body—but you are far more than these. Use the thoughts. Use the emotions. Let them pass through you as the clouds pass through a summer day. But a summer day is composed of far more than the sun and the clouds in the sky.

Now I suppose I shall have to prove that I am jolly. I will try to think of something. I do give you *(BA)* welcome.

Why is it so difficult for you to learn what freedom is?

([Theodore:] "Freedom in the total sense seems like irresponsibility almost.")

That is indeed <u>your</u> interpretation. And this is because you set demands.

Now I ask you—how far do you think a flower would get if, in the morning, it turned its face toward the sky and said, "I demand the sun?" "And now I need rain. So I demand the rain! And I need bees to come and take my pollen. So I demand the bees!" And who would it ask for these things? And it would say, our imaginary flower, "I demand discipline! I demand therefore the sun shall shine for a certain amount of hours; the rain shall pour for a certain amount of hours; and the bees shall come—bee A, C, D, E and F—and I shall accept no other bees to come. And I demand that, furthermore, that discipline operate and that the soil shall follow my command, but I do not allow the soil any spontaneity of its own—and I do not allow the sun any spontaneity of its own—and I do not agree that the sun knows what it is doing. I demand it follow my ideas of discipline!"

And who, I ask you, would listen? For in the miraculous spontaneity of the sun, there is a discipline that utterly escapes you—and a knowledge that is beyond any knowledge that we know. And in the spontaneous playing of the bees from flower to flower there is a discipline beyond any that you know, and the laws that follow their own knowledge—and joy that is beyond command. For the true discipline, you see, is found only in spontaneity. Spontaneity knows its own order, and in the spontaneous expression of each spirit—you find what you consider discipline—and there is no other.

In the spontaneous working of your nervous system, what do we find? We see here the head of the Dean that rests upon his shoulders and the intellect that demands discipline. And yet all of this rests upon the spontaneous workings of the inner self and the nervous system of which the intellect knows little. And without that spontaneous discipline, there would be no ego to sit upon the shoulders and demand discipline.

Now that I have proven how jovial I am, you may all take a break!

(Break.)

Now if you want to wear false eyelashes to class, I will come to see it. I will not keep you overlong. I can see, however, that my hardheaded lecture did some good as it was intended to do particularly in one area to my right

(Florence). To my left *(Brad)*—we still have some work to do—and I will see to it that my friend Ruburt helps us in this matter.

Now. My Dean, the spontaneous self that you so fear is the self that speaks to Bega. Then it is not a self that you have to fear. You are highly confused as to the meaning of spontaneity and discipline. Now the seasons come each year as they have come for centuries upon your planet—and they come with a magnificent spontaneity and with a creativity that bursts upon the world. And yet they come in your system within a highly ritualized and disciplined manner. And spring does not come in December. And there is a merging of spontaneity and discipline—truly marvelous to behold. And you do not fear the coming of the seasons.

Now all of you—each in your own way—contribute. For you can consider the body of the earth and all that you know—the trees and the seasons and the sky—to some extent as your own contribution—the combination of spontaneity and discipline that gives fruit to the earth.

(Break.)

([Jane:] "I got this fantastic image of everybody spontaneously forming all these seasons and everything. And there was a tremendous effort involved individually to get spring going—to get the buds out...that the good things that we do that we don't realize...you know we think of war—and we see all the evil we do; and that the good things we do, we often don't realize—and that we actually form the seasons—the

spring, the other seasons; and that the earth itself, the physical earth, is like the Garden of Eden in our subconscious. That is, it's a result of the good things that we do that we maintain—that we create and maintain this fantastic planet that we get our sustenance and food from—and everything else. And that when spring comes, it's a creative—a tremendous achievement—on the part of each individual on the earth and in this section of the country, because we have done it. And our belief in spontaneity and life and vitality has actually helped form this. Different chemicals come out through our systems that we don't even know of that change the atmosphere and so forth and brings all this about. "

(The preceding paragraph was stated by Jane while she still remained in a semi-trance state. The trances this night were exceedingly deep and she had more than usual difficulty "surfacing."

(The class discussed the Cornell University crisis [the armed "take-over"], including some facts which had previously appeared in the various media in distorted form.)

Now. I will wish you a fond good evening so that you know you can leave when you like. Not that you would not leave when you are ready to go.

I have told you before, however, that there is never any justification for violence. There is never any justification for threats. It makes no difference whether or not you think that the end justifies the means because it does not.

The means creates the end.

And if the means are violent, the ends are violent.

None of you—none of you—including our profound Dean, solidly understands what I am trying to tell you. I hope you shall some day.

You create your own physical reality!

Each of you individually creates the reality that you know—and en masse, altogether, you create the reality of your world and your universe. There is no good within it in which you do not participate—and there is no evil within it in which you do not participate—and in which you have no part.

Now this is practical and it is the only real practicality. For if you hate, you create a hateful reality. And to the extent that you hate, you find reality hateful. To the extent that you fear, you create a fearful reality. To the extent that you love, you create a lovely reality. To the extent that you create, you create a reality full of creativity—and this is my message.

ESP CLASS SESSION, MAY 6, 1969
TUESDAY

(Notes by Jane from Dr. Joseph Murphy's The Power of Your Subconscious Mind.

(The power of your subconscious is enormous. It inspires you, guides you, reveals to you names and facts and scenes from the storehouse of memory. It started your heartbeat, controls circulation of your blood, regulates digestion, assimilation, and elimination. When you eat a piece of bread, your subconscious transmutes it into tissue, muscle, bone and blood

Your subconscious controls all the vital processes and functions of your body.

(It never sleeps or rests. You can discover the miracle-working power of the subconscious by plainly stating to your subconscious mind, prior to sleep, that you wish a specific thing accomplished. Here then is a source of power and wisdom that places you in touch with omnipotence, or the power that moves the world, guides the planets in their course, and causes the sun to shine. Your subconscious mind is the source of your ideals, aspirations and altruistic urges.

(Whatever thoughts, beliefs, opinions, theories or dogma you write, engrave or impress on your subconscious mind—you will experience them as the objective manifestation of circumstances, conditions and events; what you write on the inside, you experience on the outside.

(It is a universal truth that whatever you impress on your subconscious mind is expressed on the screen of space as condition, experience and event. Thought is incipient action. The reaction is a response from your subconscious mind which corresponds with the nature of your thought. Your subconscious mind can be likened to the soil which can grow all kinds of seeds, good or bad. Every thought is a cause and every condition an effect.

(As you sow in your subconscious mind, so shall you reap in your body and environment. Whatever your conscious mind assumes and believes to be true, your subconscious mind will accept and bring to pass. Whatever you habitually think sinks into the subconscious. The subconscious is the seat of the emotions and is a creative mind. Once subconscious accepts

an idea, it begins to execute it. Whatever you feel is true, your subconscious will accept and bring forth into experience.)

When he *(Theodore)* gets the gold tassel, I will pin it on him.

My friend Ruburt has been correct, however, and we must have a tighter ship! And I will see to it that we have one. I do not see your party faces—you had them on earlier. You may sing "Happy Birthday" to me—I will give you a list of my birthdays and you can have a party at every class!

Now, I am only speaking because many of you have known that I was here. And it ill behooves me not to bid you welcome when you felt my presence. But in many of your discussions, there has only been surface thought and surface feelings—and we do not walk on the surface in this class. I would push your heads collectively and individually underneath—for you still do not understand that you create your physical reality! You form your blocks and shove them up upon the surface of the earth. You cannot solve the problems of your world on a surface level. If you could, you would have done it centuries ago. You must step out of your present perspective in order to see your world clearly. Here you are not to hide within the closet of three-dimensionality and cry, "It is dark and I cannot see!" and refuse to use the inner light that can alone aid your vision.

ESP CLASS SESSION, MAY 20, 1969
TUESDAY

(The Rev. John Cross and wife, Mabel were guests for the evening. Jane introduced Jack as a "rock drummer." His presence was advanced as a possible reason for the quietness of the class.)

And I thought you were on your good behavior because I was here. I will have to learn to be a reverend rock drummer—and I will keep the beat with you.

Now, I bid you welcome. They are not at their best this evening for you are a minister and they are frightened.

He seems like a very nice gentleman to me. You do not have to be so intimidated.

Our Lady from Florence over here is filled with questions that she would ask you. The questions tumble from her mind indeed like heavy blocks. And yet, you have not asked them. He is a good one to answer them for you. And he has answers for them.

Now we have been sliding along again. Our Lady from Florence has made some progress for, since I spoke to you last, you finally took me to heart. I hoped for more from you—and you will surprise yourself. I am speaking to our young merchant from Venice over here *(to Daniel McIntyre).*

Our other friend *(Brad)* is playing with his crutches—tossing them in the air a bit—practicing a two-step without them. But we need more than that. You have book one of the material. I tell you that that information is practical information. You can put it to use. I am flattered that you pick it up and look at it now and then. You may have it bound in gold or leather and keep it as a keepsake. But it will do you little good unless you use it.

You must become more aware of your inner selves—they are not all that horrible. You still fear, as our Lady of Florence, that there is a cellar door—a cellar door to your mind—to your inner self. And, if you open it, all sorts of demons will emerge. And if there are any angels, the demons will gobble them up before you ever get to see them. Instead, I tell you, as I have told you before, you are more than you know. And it is up to *you* to find your own reality. I cannot give it to you. I can point you in the direction—but the experience is personal and the experience is subjective and the journey is one that you must make and that you must make alone. I cannot make it for you. I have my own journeys to make...and detours here. And any problems that you have I have had them—so look at me and know how indestructible you are!

I tell you now—and for the sake of our guests—that death is not sober and it is not death. You simply take a giant step forward. And as my friends know that I will, I will tell you that all vitality rings...and it rings through this frame and it rings through your own frame—and it is lighthearted; and it is joyful; and it knows not sobriety; as you know, it is a lighthearted thing.

Consciousness left to itself is like April left to itself. It is *you* who project disasters into the month of April—whenever disasters occur. And it is you who projects disasters into consciousness when those disasters occur.

I use Ruburt's body, with his permission, because he is a friend of mine. You use your own bodies—they are the vehicles that you wear. As Ruburt would say, they're the space garments you don in order to dwell upon your earth. They are not you—you use them—use them joyfully and gladly and well but do not identify with them for they are not you. I have used and discarded more bodies than I would desire to count. And had I really died with even one of those bodies, I would not be speaking to you now—and you would not be sitting beside me. For you have also spoken with many tongues.

But again, coming here once a week may help you find yourself—it may point you in the right direction—but you will only find yourself when you journey inward. And by journeying inward I do not mean a quick and hasty and apologetic trip to your child memories. I do not mean an attempt to find out why you are frightened of spiders or have boils on your arm. I am speaking of a more extensive journey. And all of you know to what I am referring.

Open up the gates of your consciousness while you sleep! You know you are more than what you refer to as your "conscious I," but you should know it through <u>experience</u>! Open up the barriers in your daily lives—step outside of the self that you know—and you will solve your difficulties! You will solve them and you will know that you have done so. You will know that the ability is within yourself and you have used it—then you may hit me over the head with your crutches and I will laugh!

I will let you return to your social discourse.

(Break.)

You may ask me any questions that you like. I do not guarantee that I will answer them all. But I will answer some of them.

([Jack Cross:] "When we leave the physical body, where do we go?")

You go where you want to go. Now. When your ordinary, conscious, waking mind is lulled in like your sleep state, you travel in other dimensions. You are already having experience within those other dimensions. You are preparing your own way. When you die, you go into those ways which you have prepared. There are various periods of training that vary according to the individual.

You must understand the nature of reality before you can manipulate within it intelligently and well. In this environment and in physical reality, you are learning—you are supposed to be learning—that your thoughts have reality and that you create the reality that you know. When you leave this dimension, then you concentrate upon the knowledge that you have gained. If you still do not realize that you create the reality that you know, then you return and again you learn to manipulate and again and again you see the results of your own inner reality as you meet it objectified. You teach yourself the lesson until you have learned it.

And when you have learned it, then you have begun to learn how to handle the consciousness that is yours intelligently and well. And then you can form images for the benefit of others and lead them and guide them. And then you can continue, you can continue to enlarge the scope of your understanding and consciousness—and as you do this, you take on a more conscious awareness of your responsibility. And your responsibility is not difficult to understand.

([Jack Cross:] "What determines the time between reincarnations?")

You. If you are very tired, then you rest. If you are wise, you take time to digest your knowledge and to plan your next life even, you see, as a writer plans a next book. If you have too many ties with this reality and if you are too impatient, and if you have not learned sufficiently, then you may return too quickly.

It is always up to the individual. There is no predestination. And there is no one who tells you what you must do. The answers are within yourself then as the answers are within yourself now.

([Jack Cross:] "How do you discover those answers for yourself?")

Now there are many ways—but only one real way. And the way is to begin the journey, as Ruburt told you, into the nature of your own consciousness for the answers are within you and not out from you—and no one can tell you the answers. Now in one way, each individual will find his own answer—and yet all answers, in another way, are one.

You must try to forget for a period of time each day

the self that you think of as yourself the adult pretensions, the adult bignesses. You must remember the childhood spontaneity. You must think of the freedom that is within a flower. Now, it seems to you that a flower cannot move, and therefore has no freedom. And yet I tell you, you must think about the freedom of a flower.

You must dissociate yourself from the person that you know. Close your eyes. Imagine anything that you like that is pleasant to you. It makes no difference what it is. Then imagine yourself stepping apart from yourself in whatever way you choose. And then imagine that all about you there is another dimension and you need only take one step at a time—and you will find your answers. You have only to begin. There is an adventure and it is within you. And there are answers, and they are within you—and you can find them. Now. You have more questions?

([Jack Cross:] "How do you develop the power of spiritual healing?")

You already have the power of spiritual healing. You want to know how to use it. Now you use it whether or not you know that you do. When you think thoughts of peace and vitality, and when you wish a man well, then you help heal him.

Now in order to direct this power consciously, you must again get used to the feeling of your own subjective experience—so that you can tell subjectively when this energy is pouring through you and outward. You can use your imagination and imagine perhaps that you hold an arrow and want to direct it to a proper location. But with practice, there is a subjective knowing that you will recognize and understand. But you use the ability whether you realize you use it or not. You are a healer, whether you realize this or not.

Now. I have some questions. It is more difficult for me to form questions than for me to answer them. My question is this—and you do not need to answer it now. You do not need to answer it at any time, to me. It is a question for yourself:

Would you not be freer to pursue your work out of the framework with which you are now involved?

([Jack Cross:] "You mean the church?")

I do, indeed. Not <u>the</u> church—but <u>any</u> church. Do not your ideas already leap over the fences and the fields? And do you not already feel hampered within the environment in which you have spent so much time? And are you not only now—and even reluctantly—taking small steps where you would take giant steps? You do not need to answer.

([Jack Cross;] "Yes, I will answer that. Yes, it <u>is</u> true.")

Your answers to the questions that you gave me will come from within. They will come in an easier fashion if you can free yourself. For you have formed barriers without knowing it—where barriers do not exist.

Now. I will let you return to what I hope is pleasant social discourse.

([Jack Cross:] "It has been very pleasant.")

I have enjoyed it.

([Jack Cross:] "So have we. Thank you.").

Now, dear friends, you all dwell in the same unlimited dimension—you simply have not opened your eyes to see it. You think that you are blind and so you do not see. The universe in which I dwell is the universe in which all of you dwell. Some of you have better eyesight than others and the vision is not physical. Now. You have done well with theories *(addressing Rev. Cross);* now, I tell you to forget them. Forget the self that has the theories—and begin to <u>experience</u>. To do this, follow the directions that I have given, but also get in the habit of looking about you morning, noon and night—and realizing that there is more within every environment than each small room that you see.

Realize that there are personalities that you cannot see physically, yet they are there. And look positively for them. Realize that there are voices you cannot hear with your physical ears, and listen for them inwardly.

Now. I have been, in my many pasts, an intellectual gentleman and a frivolous female. And yet I will tell you, that as a frivolous female who loved to play with a ball in the bright afternoon and had no chores to perform, seemingly an idle life and seemingly a quite useless personality—I was not burdened with intellect—and yet in that one particular life I learned more about the nature of spontaneity and joy than in many of my ponderous intellectual existences.

The trick is not to try too hard, to realize that the answers are available, that they are there, that you can find them. All that is necessary is given to the flower. And all that you want will be given to you, but you must want what you want desperately enough, wholeheartedly enough. An intellectual curiosity will give you some answers but it will not give you the deepest answers.

You must be willing, quite willing, not only willing but <u>anxious </u>to travel in dimensions that you are not acquainted with on an egotistical basis.

And into this reality you do not go as a grown man with preconceived ideas. You go as a wonderer without preconceptions. And you become acquiescent and the answers are given to you—and to you—and to you.

IMPRESSIONS
(FOR JACK AND MABEL CROSS)
MAY 20, 1969 (BY JANE ROBERTS)

Fourteenth-Century France—riding academy—saw riding accident by an academy when you were about 14— you were held up, crippled in some way, for a couple of years—you had a brother and the brother was with you at the time of the accident.

I saw a brick structure—don't know whether or not it was a riding academy—had a very wide entrance— related to the accident mentioned before.

You had a brief life as twins—some definite clear-cut divisions within yourself, have to do with this life when you were one of two—one going one way, and one going the other—one twin had a strong leaning toward military things—a soldier—the organization of the church now serves the same purpose, I believe—security within the organization—the twin who was in the military found his sense of identity as a soldier within the system, but he had great faith in the system—in what he was doing—the other twin was more given to a statesman-like sort of thing—and was in fact an orator, although he had another profession—it included oration to people—the two of you had a very strong telepathic relationship—and this time the church has provided the same kind of organization—you sort of resented the fact that this twin brother of yours had this organization in which he found support and in which he felt so a part because he was absolutely certain of the aims and goals of the organization and he was a good soldier within it—and at that time you envied him that security and that sense of identity within the system in which he believed. This time the orator part of you is still strong in that you want to teach and like to talk and to discuss issues—but also at the same time you wanted the sense of security that you felt the other brother had—also you picked up his desire to go to battle for, only in this case you are using battle for ideas that you are struggling for. The other brother was battling for what the organization wanted, and served the organization well—you are now battling the things the organization wants and you feel the division—this division is bringing up memories subconsciously, in this past life where there was this division between you and your brother.

Greek name—Ostinatious—I am getting also 12 BC—this would be his name, not the other twin, that is because he had this telepathic communication with his twin, he has this sense of wanting unity within himself very strongly, at the same time a sense of being divided. A strong inclination to go ahead independently with his ideas, balanced by the desire to find security within the system, and the fear to leave it. His intellectual freedom, he feels, exists only so long as it is cushioned by the feeling of security of the organization—and if he cut loose he would be too panic-stricken to be an independent thinker, leading to a dilemma which you reached just after 30 in this life. You, Mabel, were the twin brother.

ESP CLASS SESSION, JUNE 3, 1969 TUESDAY

(Brad's Note: the first few words [by Seth] were not recorded.)

...to solve your problems and triumph over your challenges—and the impetus is this: You must not journey into inner reality until you feel secure in <u>physical</u> reality—for you cannot live in two worlds at once unless you are secure in one. You need a firm groundwork—a groundwork that you can trust. And then you can travel through these other doors, but you must be able to stand on your two feet in this universe—and then you will go consciously where your body cannot follow and you will find your answers. But you must have something secure to hang on to. Now there is no better reason to solve your problems.

When you are certain that you feel at least reasonably secure, where you are, then we shall take you to where you are not and you will find yourself. You are already there, but in order to go there, you must start from somewhere. You must start with, you see, a balance and a degree of security—you must start with confidence. And if you travel too quickly and too far, you will not have confidence. For in the back of your mind you will think: If I do not feel secure in physical reality, then why should I feel secure here—and you will not have the daring that is necessary, nor will you have the peace of mind—and the peace of mind is the key to the door.

So when you are on the way to solving your situation here, I will give you some new ones to solve—and I will give you a push along the way, and you can count on it—and you can count on it when you tell me that you are making true progress here. Then I will give you a gigantic push.

(The above was addressed to Brad. Brad's recorder failed to record a part of the above, and in ascertaining what portion was missed, a short burst of singing emanated from the recorder's previously used tape. Seth reappeared and said the following:)

If I could sing that beautifully, I would sing for you through our classes. Now I wish you *(Daniel)* a bon voyage. And I did not mean to hurt your *(class)* feelings; far be it from me to hurt your feelings when you hurt your own so well you do not need help from me. I will have a message for you *(Florence)* through our friend Ruburt shortly in any case. I simply wanted you to know that I was here and I did have a specific message that I wanted to deliver to our friend *(Brad)* on this side. And if you do not have the words recorded, they are recorded there *(pointing to Brad's head)* and you will not forget them. And when I make promises I make promises and I keep them. And when I say I will give a "push" at a certain time, I will give a <u>fine</u> push... though then you may not need it. I've come through this evening in any case simply as a friend. I wish you all well. I am not going to keep you until two o'clock in your morning. Some evening I will keep you until two o'clock in the morning just so you can say that I have done it. But you would not bless me the following morning—of that I am sure.

(At this point, Theodore said; "I am in good shape tonight, Seth, I'm ready.")

Now, indeed you are. And—as a piece or chunk of physical matter—you are indeed immediate and here. You do not understand the ways in which you project the physical matter of yourself into this room, however. When you understand that completely and fully, you will no longer be within physical reality. But that is of little notice. You will never notice the difference. In any reality, you create the image that you see. And the reality that follows this one will seem as physical to you as this—and as real. But you will have freedoms within it that you do not have now—not unless at 8 o'clock in the morning you leap from the rooftops and fly through the windows to your death.

You can do things with the inner image that you cannot do with the physical image. But while you are doing them, they appear physical. Do you follow me?

Now. In this existence, when you see a picture in your mind, and when there is strong emotion and vivid desire behind it, it will be constructed. There will be a time lapse within this system, but in other systems there may be no time lapse—and your thought may be instantly transposed into reality. Therefore, now you must learn the nature of your thoughts and how to handle energy.

([Theodore:] "Because now we have time to do it.")
Indeed.

([Theodore:] "But between the time of thinking about it now and the time it becomes a reality, other thoughts can come to bear on that idea and change it before it becomes a reality. Is that so?")

Then the ideas merge.

([Theodore:] "I see, and form a compromise—composite.")

Now as a compromise, but not as a composite. I will leave you, but I will give you more information on that topic the next time we meet. And I will keep my eye on you *(Daniel)*, but I will not bear tales.

(Break.)
(Summary for Jane:
([Theodore:] "He talked some more about physical

matter—and elaboration on the things we've talked about during the evening. The reality on another plane or in another dimension is just as physical as what we experience as physical here—just as real, seems physical to them. But the freedoms are greater, so that when we think of something on another plane, it happens instantaneously. Whereas here, there is a time lag between the time we think of something and it results in a created action or object. In the time lag on this plane, there are other thoughts, projections on the same idea or object; Seth declined to go into their effects on the final idea or object until a later time.

("By projecting our thoughts to this finished product, we can influence our health, our future, our position, etc. We should picture ourselves as <u>being</u> in a state of good health. Now I would assume that this same thing applies to a station or vocation... ")

... But never as a finished product. For a state of health is not an end product—or an unchanging station in those terms. It is the ability to effectively handle energy in a constructive way for your own benefit and the benefit of others. The state of health is a poor term. You should indeed imagine yourself, therefore, able to handle your energy effectively for your own good and the good of others; to imagine yourself as a channel through which the creativity of the universe can express itself. For when you harbor negative ideas and resentments, then indeed you set up a block and the block causes distortions. Now you call them illnesses in many instances. They are distortions. The energy is being distorted and misused and misshapen.

([Theodore:] "But to want good health or position just for the sake of that is not the end of the line. That, you are saying, is just the beginning of...")

It is a <u>beginning</u>, and health is not a static state in any case...

([Theodore:] "We should desire good health because it makes it possible for us to do something else—to serve or perform some other role—")

You should desire good health because it is a natural state of your being. You should trust in the innate intelligence of your own being—which produces good health. Health is a natural state of your being. Through your physical image the energy of the universe expresses itself. You as an individualized consciousness are a part of this, and you cannot express yourself fully nor fulfill your purpose as an identity, as an individual, if you are not in good health—for the effects of the body are felt in the mind...and the effects of the mind are felt in the body. You distort the picture.

Now I did not intend a question-and-answer service this evening, but I seem to be involved in one. And some evening I will turn the tables. And when I ask you questions, I will expect some answers. And they will not be easy questions—and they will not be general questions. And I will make you search for the answers—and the answers will form steps upon which you can walk and will serve as foundations within which you can travel within yourselves. But they will be <u>your</u> answers and not <u>my</u>

answers.

([Theodore:] "Now it has been suggested that the next time I go to New York I might see a man...")

It is <u>indeed</u> possible!

([Theodore:]"But the point is—I guess the question I'm asking is: Am I really more interested in the certain possibilities of status, and that would not be the positive way of looking at things—or should I be seeing that man within a framework of, just as we were talking about health as just being a stepping stone, should I be seeing this man with a viewpoint towards what this can mean for helping other people be part of a constructive arrangement?")

You have answered your own questions. Your latter statement applies.

Now, I will bid you a fond good evening—particularly to our Merchant from Venice *(to Daniel)* who is going to travel afar.

There are other ways to travel, and we will see that you learn of them. There are other fascinations and foreign countries upon your planet, but it is good that you learn of those also. We will get you used to the idea of foreign lands and then we will teach you to travel into lands that are <u>really</u> foreign—and we will give you an idea of the vocabulary used—and it will not be as simple as "good morning" and "good evening" or "where can I find a can of beans?"

(Pause. [Theodore:] "My interpretation of what he said is that (1) good health is a natural part of ourselves, and so we should naturally desire it, and (2) good health in itself is

not the objective at all. It is what you can do when you are in a state of good health. We carried it into another dimension besides health...vocational aspects. We project ourselves ahead mentally to vocational status we are interested in, and by doing that, accomplish it. It is not the status itself that is the end. It is what we are able to do through it, that we should really be aiming at."

([Dan:] "Theodore made the analogy of health vs. occupation. His implication was that the product of good health was the ability to do good more efficiently. Taking it over into occupations, then, I don't know how it would be—advances an occupation, I guess, is the closest."

([Theodore:]"...Choice or advancement—and advancement maybe."

Now I am going to leave you. However, I want to clear up an issue. If you are in poor health, this does not mean that you are an evil person. It means that you have a block in that particular area in which you are unable to utilize energy constructively. And if you are not at the top of your profession, the same thing applies. It does not follow that those in excellent health are more blessed than others. It does mean that in that particular area they are able to utilize energy more effectively.

And theoretically, <u>theoretically</u>, if you are using energy the way you should, you would indeed be at the top of your profession and in excellent health and filled with abundance. Now various kinds of lacks can show up in many ways—in mental deficiencies—a man or a woman who has strong and definite mental deficiencies—

who has strong negative habits—such a person has blocks in those areas. You may not attain perfection now—I have not attained it. But it is the ideal toward which we must work.

I do not want you to have the attitude, however, or make the implication, that your health or status in any way automatically, and alone, is an indication of your spiritual wealth—or lack of it.

Some of you, for example, do well in certain areas and are blocked in others. We want to get rid of the blocks. You are working toward this ideal, and the ideal is—and you will achieve it—to use all your abilities, all of your capabilities—and in doing this, you will help others automatically. And you will help the race of which you are a part. And you will add to the creativity of All That Is and I said that you would add to it. This is for you, for the anticipated argument that you will think of *(to Florence)*.

And now I do wish you a fond good evening.

And store up your questions—and store up your answers—for I will grade you! You have been involved in <u>this</u> examination for many years!

SESSION 494, ESP CLASS SESSION, JULY 15, 1969, TUESDAY

(*This was taken from the regular session file. The ESP class filed in Box 4 of the Jane Roberts Papers archived at Yale University is the same except it does not include Rob's notes.*

SESSION 7/15/1969

(Notes by Rob: Some of Seth's voice effects were very loud. I heard Seth rather clearly through 2 closed doors after I had retired. The session began late—about 11:30 PM and lasted well over an hour.

(The session is included in the regular series [Session 494] because of the voice effects; the fact that both Seth and his entity spoke; some new ideas from both entities; and because no regular session was held the next day, Wednesday, July 16.

(The data re the paintings—Bega—Theodore M., was interesting, etc. On July 17, Theodore purchased the painting of Bega as designated by Seth. On July 16, Ned and Sue Watkins bought the oils of Charlie Painter, the dream hands, and Moses.

(Very late in the evening, Ned Watkins woke me to express concern because of the length of the session tonight—at perhaps 1 AM or later. Jane then was speaking for Seth's entity. Ned and others were concerned that Jane couldn't exert enough control to come out herself.

(Jane called back to me that she was all right during a break, and this and my waking up served to end the session. Jane said she felt it was a good session, an unusual occasion to get some new ideas, so she went along with Seth and his entity. She also knew the whole session was being recorded.)

You will have your tales, but tonight is not the night of telling. Now. I have been here and I have not intruded, because you are learning to collect and use energy on your own. I did indeed however stand in front of each one of you and looked into your faces and you did not see me. It is some experience to stand before another and see no comprehension in his face—but I am used to it. Now. You *(Jane and Sue)* used your energy like a ball that a child plays with, both you and Ruburt. And you tossed it back and forth, but you did not collect and direct it properly, and we shall have to give you lessons. But you shall do the work.

(To Brad:) Now I am sitting here for my portrait. You may indeed get only our friend Ruburt. But then you may get more than your friend Ruburt. The camera may be comprehending or it may not be comprehending.

I do not like to interrupt you in the beginning of your summer... *(unintelligible)*... however... Far be it from me to interrupt when you are not working; when you are not looking within yourselves. The summer season within yourselves is far more enjoyable than the summer streets down which you walk. But far be it from me to mention that you have not been working.

And when I do ask the questions, and I shall ask them, I shall expect some ready answers. When you immerse yourselves completely in physical reality, then you have no time for the inner voice.

([Theodore:] "That is what I'm doing.")

It is your loss. Now, there is a way—when you are involved in physical activity, and even intense mental work—to change the inner focus so that you are aware of two realities at once and can manipulate quite easily in the physical reality as you must. Now, you ask your Bega—for I have told him the message and I have told him to tell

SESSION 7/15/1969

you. We shall see how good he is. And I want to know what he tells you for I want to see how he is delivering my suggestions.

([Theodore:] "Is that Bega on the wall?")

Now I ask you, what would Bega be doing on the wall?

([Theodore:] "You are on the wall.")

I am painted on the wall.

Now your friend has been here this evening as a student, but not exactly the same kind of a student as you are—he is a practice teacher.

You *(Sue)* lost some good bets this evening. And you *(Ned)* lost many good bets this evening. Now. There is a difference between passivity and alert passivity. And you need to learn the difference. <u>Here</u> you need to learn the difference. Again, I welcome our new member *(Lydia)*.

([Lydia:] "Did you give me the bump on the head?")

Far be it from me to bump fair ladies on the head! The bump, for this has been a very active evening, was from your playful poltergeist AA. I have better things to do than to bump maidens or madams on the head.

Now. You must realize that within this room, and within any room, at any time there are other personalities that you do not perceive. There are ways of perceiving them <u>if</u> they choose to be perceived. Possibly, with some help from certain directions, we shall see what we can do in other classes. And our friend Ruburt is quite correct, you *(Brad)* learn the nature of the inner self first—and <u>then</u> we shall help you in the development of your own abilities. And before too long, we will have a message for you to take to heart.

I have come through simply to let you know that I have been here, and to let you know that I know that you are sliding through the summer.

(To Sue and Ned:) I do have one point to make. The child *(Sean)* was a girl—1432—France—and at one time your sister—strong literary abilities—some interest in music—should not be pampered for the personality is already given to indulgence. There may be an allergy to wheat—early in life—was also known to this one here in Spain—the country now called Spain—in 801 as an uncle—then a warrior-type personality—but again given to indulgence.

An entity on a par with the parents. A mole or mark on one of the feet—a possible weak point in the right elbow—given to high exuberance, quick moods—but not forgiving. The personality should not be indulged, but it should not be shown dissonance—and discipline should be fair, for it will hold grudges otherwise.

I had meant to mention earlier that your daughter and sister were brothers in a previous life in Afghanistan. You *(Sally)*, I believe, 1541-1583, a rug-maker, their father—that is, you were their father. There was also another child—and that child will be G's husband in this life. There will be a close connection, then, between the two of you—but also a sense of rivalry. Your mother was a very heavy-handed father to you in that existence. Your father has now strong feminine traits because in Boston in an immediately past life there was a woman—give us a moment—the first name was also Lillian. The last name—your vice-president to the contrary—was Agnew. There are records of this particular existence twenty-five miles, approximately, west of Boston—at that time, a small town... three children who died before the age of three, and records, I believe, attesting to this fact—couched in one of the historical societies—or in land grant information.

Now. We will try to have a session for you *(Brad)*, our friend Brad the Bull, shortly—and clear up some of your difficulties—for some of them are because you are bull-headed. You will not let the inner self speak clearly enough to you—so we will give it the voice that you can hear... and you will know when we have the session, you—will intuitively realize, that what we say is true—and there is no need to fight what you are fighting—and the secret that you try so hard to hide from your conscious mind is not that terrible a secret. There is some past life that operated in your case that has caused a block, and we hope that we can help you remove it. Bulls can rip down fences.

Now, I will let my friend—*(laugh from Ned)*—you, as Ruburt would say, you are looking for it! And those who look for it in this room, get it. The portrait is a portrait of Ruburt as a woman in one of the past lives mentioned—and in that particular instance, as a grandmother of twelve children. Strongly gifted psychically—given to hovering in dark forests—and a midwife. Now, he does not know this, so I will give you the honor of telling him.

I will now let our friend take a rest. And you may rest if you are up to it.

Now, I will tell you *(Theodore)* something. Bega is there and I will let <u>you</u> tell me which portrait is his. You may ask Bega or tell me. But you did not pick the correct portrait. *(Theodore commented that one was "too much Hebrew.")*

Bega has had many lives—do not limit yourself in your thinking—do not limit yourself in your feelings—and do not retreat in the summertime from your inner self.

Now. There has been energy present in this room, and <u>strong energy</u>, this evening. But you have not been serious enough about using it, nor have you been playful enough to use it without serious note. You may use it in two ways, you see. You may play with it and use it marvelously—or you may use it seriously—but <u>in between</u> you will not use it at all, for you cannot harness it. And in your own daily activities, in your playful moments, you can almost achieve the freedoms that the inner self knows. And in your most serious moments, you can almost achieve the freedom that the inner self knows. But in your mundane moments, you will not achieve it. And when you half try, you will not achieve it.

(Theodore holding up a portrait.) That is not Bega! I want you to seriously consider each one of the paintings and tell me which one is Bega!

Now. I do not want to see another painting. I do not want an attitude that says, "Is this it?" I want an intuitive feeling on your part and a recognition. Do you intuitively feel that that is a portrait of Bega?

([Theodore:] "The one I thought was Bega was actually Ruburt.")

We are sorry about that! I never liked wine—I always liked brandy—and no one brings it to me—and Ruburt does not drink it.

([Brad:] "I will bring you some last week [sic].")

But how will you get Ruburt to drink it? I always liked a warm brandy even on a summer's night.

Now. What is your *(Theodore)* intuitive feeling? Now I want you to look at the portrait. Close your eyes. How much reality does the portrait have for you? Can you see it in your mind's eye?

([Theodore:] "Yes, I can see it with the feeling of a friend.")

That is because it is the portrait of Bega. But you did not pick it out as your first choice. Now, Bega has been here as I have been here and he was calling you to look toward the corner of the room—and you were too intellectually smug to do so as Ruburt is often too intellectually smug to do what I ask him to do. And your own intellectual ideas prevented you from first picking out your intuitive choice, as far as the portraits were concerned.

Now. There is someone else who has been here and who is connected with our new student. But our new student does not know this person—it is no one with whom she has previously communicated. Because she was not ready. This personality is also a student of mine and a practice teacher.

Now, <u>you see what you are willing to see</u>, and it is stupidity to consider suggestion as the result or the cause of what you see. It is stupidity in class to worry that suggestion would cause a given result—for suggestion causes whatever you see. You form your physical reality through suggestion and expectation. You experience what you expect to experience at a subconscious <u>and</u> a conscious level. And therefore, as Ruburt is very careful that suggestion is not involved, so he has also had you be overly cautious, and there have been many opportunities in class that you have missed for this reason—and these are the bets that I have spoken about earlier this evening. You have the ability to see more than you saw and <u>you </u>have the ability. You enjoyed your passivity *(to Ned)* to the point of an enjoyous giving-up; and instead, you see, there is a point within passivity where you are passively alert. And you went beyond the point and lost what you might have seen. As our friend here went beyond the point *(referring to Theodore)*, looked at the portraits and consciously—for you did not make an original, intuitive, judgment—but <u>consciously </u>looked at these portraits in terms of nationality, age and all the requirements that you thought of.

Now again, let me tell you, <u>though the hour be late</u> *(quite loudly)* and though Ruburt thinks that such demonstrations as these are hardly worth the effort *(quite softly)* and childish endeavors at best, I still want you to know, as I always want you to know, that my vitality is your own and that the energy that swings through this small frame is but an echo of the energy that swings through your own personality.

I have said before that you have lived many lives and that you can know these existences within yourself. I am not afraid that we shall be kicked out of our apartment. And I also am quite sure that as you grow to know Ruburt and as you grow to know me you will realize that there is a difference in our personalities and that indeed when I tell you that my vitality spans both space and time, then you will know that I know whereof I am speaking. And that this vitality is your own—then feel it within yourselves—now it is being used simply to let you know of its existence, but realize that it is within <u>you</u> for <u>you</u> to use as you will—for your own good—and you *(Brad)* are not powerless. I have no body and I am not powerless, how, therefore, can you feel helpless, or you, or any of you?

My vitality is no more—no more than your own. I come to you from a long way. But the essence of yourself is not of this place nor of this time. Now, I could keep up a demonstration such as this for hours, if only to let you realize that this is your own energy—that the energy that I show is your own—you have this energy and this vitality.

(Very loud.) Now, in your terms, I am dead! How can you then be less lively? Why is it that I must tell you what vitality is when, in your terms, I am a gray ghost that flits through the darkness of the night—a face that peers through second story windows *(in reference to Sue's being*

frightened by a face that appeared at her window recently) and meets with no response but a sigh of horror. I visit my friends and they nearly faint. *(Sue apologized.)* Apologies always come later.

(Discussion.)

I said: "In your terms, I was dead;" in my terms, I am forever lively. *(This to clarify a point being discussed by the class.*

(Seth tried to break through again.
([Jane:] "What a minute."
([Ned:] "One at a time in the body.")

Now, Ruburt's abilities were so strong since childhood that he feared using them. And so I am quite used to that development. On the other hand, I wanted someone with a strong enough ego structure to contain what will amount to 40 years of mediumistic stability. I needed a personality who would be able to maintain psychological stability.

Now, I have maintained psychological stability for centuries so I find it not too much to ask that our friend Ruburt maintain it for a mere forty years. And we expect <u>you</u> *(Ned)* to maintain it and before you get the idea, again, of leaving physical reality before your chores are done, I will give you the boot from the other end.

([Ned:] "Was that you that she saw in the window the other night?")

I use many forms and if you do not like them, I am sorry. Next time I shall be a willowy, spiritual, young woman, treading very softly and I shall sing "Ave Maria"

SESSION 7/15/1969

as the glorious sun sinks in the west...and I shall tippy-toe to your window. And then from this light and spiritual form, I will bellow.

Now, there are two simple requests that I have made. One—I have been asking Ruburt to stop smoking cigarettes, a dirty habit, and smoke cigars—and he will not do so.

([Brad:] "What brand would you like?")

A fat one.

What I want you to know is this: I come here, I hope, as an endearing personality with characteristics that you understand. Now these characteristics have been mine and they <u>are</u> mine, and I am who I say I am. And yet, the Seth that you know and that you find so endearing and understandable, is but a small portion of my reality—the portion that can relate with you most easily.

It is a portion that has been physical. It is a portion that can understand your *(Theodore)* being overwhelmed with work; it is a portion that can understand your being full with child *(Sue)*; it is a portion that can understand the times when you wanted to leave physical reality *(Ned)*; it is a portion that can understand the part of you *(Sally)* that wanted to be a star; it is a portion that can understand the part of you that wanted to conquer and is afraid to conquer *(Brad)*; it is a portion that can understand the guilt you *(Rose)* feel for no reason. It is a portion that can understand the aspirations that you *(Lydia)* were unable to fulfill and if you have fulfilled them, you would not be looking into the subjects that you are looking into now.

You would not feel the need to look for answers. It is a part that can understand why you *(Vera)* have so related to this man; it is a part that can understand why the five- and seven-and eight- year-old girl that you were has related to this man and not independently gone on. It is a part that can understand why you let your aspirations go *(Theodore)*.

And this part that you see and that appears in this room and can show joy, and show its existence and reality; that can call to you beyond space and time; that shows such energy; that shows you what energy can blow through such a small and slight frame—that self is a small part of my reality. For some time yet, you will need its familiarity. And you will need the human characteristics that you know—and that were mine—and they are still mine, for this self of mine that I show to you does still exist and grow. But beyond that self, there is another self, and still another self of which I am fully aware. And that self can see through physical reality. And to that self, physical reality is like a breath of smoke in the air and that self does not need the characteristics that you know and find so endearing. And yet, it is not an unemotional self; it is a self that has condensed emotions and it is not distant.

(Jane later said there was a short break here, while Seth's entity prepared to come through. Jane didn't get any pyramid feeling though.

(All of the following data is by Seth's entity.)

([Seth II:]) And that self tells you that there is a reality beyond human reality, beyond human characteristics that you know—and within that reality even I am dwarfed and there is knowledge that can never be verbal. And there is experience that cannot be translated in human terms. Although this type of existence seems cold to you, it is a clear and crystal-like existence in which things are known that are beyond your comprehension, in which no time is needed, in your terms, for experience; in which the inner self condenses all human knowledge that has been received by you through your various existences and reincarnations has been coded and exists indelibly.

You exist, therefore, now within this reality as present and immediate as you are now—although, in my terms, more than fifty centuries of your time has elapsed since your seemingly present existence.

Yet, what you are is now and what your friend Seth is, is now. And it exists as light and as the impetus for other dimensions and consciousness.

Know that within your physical atoms now the origins of all consciousness still sings and that all the human characteristics by which you know yourselves, still exist within the eye of all our consciousness, never diminished, but always present. Your individualities never diminished, not only never diminished but gaining in experience.

So I am the Seth that is beyond the Seth that you know. And in me the knowledge and vitality of that Seth still rings. In your terms, I am a future Seth. But the terms are meaningless to me, for he is what I was, in your terms.

We form the reality that you know. We have spoken to you since the beginning of your time. We have inspired and helped those of your prophets who have looked to us.

There is no need to worry about your friend *(Ruburt)*. *We* want you to realize that there is more than your human reality. We want you to realize that there is consciousness without form, that there is consciousness with will and vitality that comes to you from beyond even those places that your Seth knows. We want you to realize that though it is hard for us to communicate, we spoke with your race before your race learned language. We gave you mental images and upon these images you learned to form the world that you know.

We gave you the pattern by which your physical selves are formed. We gave you the pattern by which you learned to form your physical reality. We gave you the patterns intricate, involved and blessed from which you form the reality of each physical thing you know. The most minute cell within your brain has been made from the patterns of consciousness which we have given you. We gave you the pattern upon which you formed your entire physical universe and the comprehension that exists within each cell, the knowledge that each cell has, the desire for organization was given by us. The entire webwork was initiated by us. We taught you to form the reality that you know.

(Present: Sue and Ned Watkins, Theodore Muldoon [banker], Sally Benson [librarian], Brad Lanton [artist], Rose Cafford [older, grandmotherly], Lydia Dobbs [candy store owner], Vera Muldoon, Florence McIntyre [not on attendance list] [school teacher], Rachel Clayton [not on attendance list]

[secretary].)

ESP CLASS SESSION, SEPTEMBER 2, 1969
TUESDAY

Now, I will tell you. In many ways, you are indeed children. And because you do not understand the truths and have not reached or understood the connections, it does not mean that the truths do not exist. And you must work towards them and use your mind to do so. It will not lead you astray. You can trust it—it will help you arrive at some questions.

You are playing games with yourselves. You are using your mind, but you are not using it correctly. You are using it to mask the true questions. You are setting up a game of checkers—one part of you is playing one game and another is playing another game. And I will have more to say to you.

I have told you time and time again, in class, and I tell you all again—and Ruburt has told you: <u>you form your own reality.</u> You form the world that you know and you form your own images. And there is no justification for violence. Now, the words sound simple. None of you has fully accepted them except as they apply to others. You must apply them to yourself. You must look within yourself and then apply these truths and learn from them. They are not theoretical ideas. They are realities.

You operate in accordance with these truths whether

you realize it or not. It is not enough to listen—you must look within yourself. It is not enough to play games. It is not enough to squint at yourself—to look at one motivation—to accept partially.

Do you want to know what freedom is? Then I will tell you. Freedom is the inner realization that you are an individual. That you <u>do</u> create your reality, that you <u>do</u> have the freedom and the joy and the responsibility of forming the physical reality in which you live. <u>Then</u> you can change the reality. <u>Then</u> you are free to move. <u>Then</u> you are free to misplace violence and you are free from it. You are not free when you say: "The idea works for everyone but <u>me</u>—but my symptoms are caused by something else—and when <u>I</u> am violent, different rules apply. Everyone else forms their own physical reality but not <u>me</u>—my reality is caused by heredity or environment. Every other nation, every other people form their own violence and is responsible for their own miserable condition, but my people—<u>they</u> are right! Any problems that they have are caused by other agencies beyond them." Then you are not facing yourselves individually or as a people.

You are meant to look at your physical condition—to compare it against what you want and what is good—and change the inner self accordingly. Any evils in the world are symptoms of you own inner disorders and are meant to lead you to cure them.

There is a beauty and a strength and a joy in looking within yourselves and a freedom from bondage. And

I hope that when I am finished with you all, you will taste some of that joy and freedom. You will not get it from a book. You will not get it like your chocolates *(indicating the box on the table)* wrapped up in a merry box. You will not get it by making exceptions. You will not get it by saying: "I am the exception to the rule!" You will not get it by running away from yourself. You will find this joy and this freedom by learning to look inward and by realizing that you create the reality that you know.

There are no exceptions to this rule. Your successes and your failures alike, you have yourselves created. If you would but understand, this is the truth that would make you free.

Now. I will say this over and over again—I will say it simply—and I will repeat it time and time again, until you understand intuitively what I mean. And I will say it in many ways. And again I will tell you: the energy that is behind and within me now, that energy is available to all of you and it resides within the selves of which you are composed. You have access to it. It is you who have denied the knowledge and it is you who close your eyes.

Now, I speak to you somewhat harshly, and yet all of you know that what I say is true. You must look inward and apply these truths. It does no good to look outward and apply them to others. You must take the first step and take the responsibility for yourself and then you have the freedom to change it. If you do not accept the responsibility, then you do not have the power to change. And the power to change is within you.

I have lived through many reincarnations and faced these problems and I was not free until I realized this basic truth.

I would prefer to be jolly with you. And my invisible and nonexistent heart goes out to you in understanding. But this does not mean that you are not doing yourselves a grave disservice—for you are not utilizing what you know. And each of you, in your heart, thinks you are an exception to the rule. And there are no exceptions to the rule. And I was no exception to the rule. And Ruburt is no exception to the rule.

Now I will let you rest—but I am not saying good evening.

(Break.)

You will not find truth neatly wrapped. You will not find it in the shelves of some store—and you will not find it chocolate-coated. Now, welcome to you *(Oliver F)*. I am sorry that you came in on a night when I am not at my jovial best. But if I do not call you to line, who else will call you to line? You are very poor at calling yourselves to line.

Remember that you only perceive a portion of your own reality. And remember that you only perceive a portion of my reality. Do you realize the implications if you make no effort to realize your own reality and to probe into it and to explore it and understand it? Then how do you think you can understand the nature of reality if you do not make an attempt to see the truths that are within yourself? Then why do you expect other truths to be given to you?

Words are but symbols! Words are not truths. You must seek through the words for the reality that they represent. And you must seek within yourselves for the reality that you represent. There is no security in ignorance—there is only fear.

Now I come to you often with playful characteristics—like a benign bishop who comes for a cup of tea and discusses realities with you. I come complete with characteristics that you can understand. I come complete with human characteristics to which you can relate and you can smile usually when I am here and smile when I am gone. But you must understand that they are the characteristics that I show you—there are other realities of personality and identity that are mine—just as there are other realities within your own personalities and you cannot laugh these away. You are but symbols of yourselves. I can tell you how to meet your own identities, and I have told you, but no one can make you look into yourselves. I can look within you and beyond you into the selves that you really are. I can see your potentials and your abilities and your promise—and you could see your own potentials and promise if you would open your inner eyes, if you would look within yourselves.

Each consciousness, regardless of its physical form, is filled with creativity and joy and possibilities—each is unique. You are at a certain level of development or you would not be here. Because you are at this level of development, you are ready and able to use your abilities more.

You are able to look within yourselves. There is nothing stopping you but <u>you</u>. And it is for this reason that I speak severely with you this evening.

The other personality with which you are familiar, which speaks through Ruburt, that personality seems very remote from you. It seems very different from me. This represents the distance that you have to travel—the inward distance. The vastness of the vision is within you, the road is within yourself, the truths are within yourself.

(Brad) You have no idea of the discovery that is possible for you. You can change your physical existence as you know it. And <u>you </u>can do it tomorrow morning. You have the ability to do this. Until you realize that you have this ability, you are powerless. When you realize and accept the fact that you form your physical reality, you can change it instantly—and <u>that</u> is your freedom. I cannot give it to you, but you can take it and I challenge you to do so. It is yours for the taking—freedom of action—it is yours, accept it. It brings with it not only responsibility, but joy such as you have never known. It is yours in this instant—you have only to accept it.

Now you *(Florence)* have your kindergarten class. Your children play with wooden blocks and they make houses. You play with mental blocks and you make worlds. You encourage your children in their creativity, and when they make errors and when you see that their houses will not stand, you do not kick the blocks aside in ire. You try, instead, to explain how the blocks must be placed one upon the other, or you smile at their childish efforts.

When the child does not understand what you are saying, you tell him again and again and you tell him in different ways. You realize that the child must understand the truths. You explain the truths as you know them, the best that you can. You tell stories and parables. And you speak in words that are familiar and you use baby talk when necessary. Baby talk in that you do not speak exactly as you would speak to an adult. And the baby talk is not obvious.

And so I hope the baby talk [*here*] is not obvious!!! It is time for you all to understand the material as I have given it, to use your mind. You have been in this class long enough to pass now beyond kindergarten. And I [*no*] longer feel that it serves that I speak to you in the most simple of terms. You have been here long enough now. When I speak to you, I shall therefore expect on your part some effort to understand me if necessary. I shall expect more of you, and you must expect more of yourselves.

Now the truck *(the sound of one can be heard outside on the street)* pauses at the corner. It is a method of communication—a vehicle. And in many ways I am a vehicle, for I am the means by which information is given to you. You are yourselves vehicles—as you move through experience and through moment points. Now you do not know what moment points are because I have not explained them in class and you have not read the material. But now it is time for you to be challenged. It is time for you to challenge your own mind and your own intuition. I shall cease speaking to you as kindergarten children, and I shall expect that you will cease thinking like kindergarten children.

We have been playing games for you, using pretty colors. The pretty colors that we have used have been good, they have caught your attention—as my personality captures your attention. But reality is far more than the children's blocks and the houses that they build in kindergarten.

The colors have more dimension than the simple reds and yellows that you know. Your own capabilities are ready to be used.

(To Brad.) In the last portion of my talk, in the very last portion, I was speaking directly to you.

Think of all the techniques that you use when you are teaching—the visual aids, the play principles. And then try to understand what I have been doing in this class. For we are taking, now, some steps forward. And you must take steps forward.

Now, imagine this: Within you, there are sounds, colors, sights that stretch backward into infinity. Your faces face this room, your eyes look out upon physical reality. Imagine, however, that you have innumerable faces, for our analogy. And that these faces look out into other realities quite as varied and quite as real. For this is indeed the cause. You can close your physical eyes and focus upon these other realities in which you also have your existence. And you can learn to manipulate in physical reality the better, because you understand your full potential. I challenge you to use all of your abilities and all of your senses. I challenge you to open your inner eyes, to use your minds, to use your inner intuitions. I challenge you to be yourselves and it is the greatest challenge that could be given you, and it is the only way that you will learn.

Again, my words are symbols. The inner part of you will respond to the symbols.

I tell you to wake up. None of you are beginning to use your potentials. Our Dean *(Theodore)* is beginning.

I can only begin to hint at the freedoms available to you if you will but open your eyes. You must act. You can easily open within yourselves those channels to creativity. You can use these. You can attain a true sense of identity. You have only a shadowy understanding of what the world means.

When I see the shadows that you accept as yourselves and when I see the brilliant and free identities that you are, then it is impossible for me not to speak to you in such a manner.

(The following was prompted by someone's urging Seth to hurry up and say good evening.)

<u>You</u> may say good evening. And if you prefer, you may indeed go.

Now. You do not understand. In many ways, Ruburt does not understand. And so now when I speak, I speak to him as well as to you. What I have been telling you, and what I will tell you, has been said before through the centuries. It is being said now again and those of you who come here will have reason to remember it well.

In many ways you do not understand what you are doing. And you do not understand that in which you are involved here. You do not comprehend its true meaning to you or to others. It may be as well for now that you do not.

But you are being given a road into yourselves that you would not have otherwise. And you are being given instruction that you would not have otherwise. And you were led here for a reason and you came for a reason and the reasons were yours, rather than mine.

My purpose was to <u>be</u> here, and to say what I must say.

You must begin to change the reality that you know. Theses ideas must go through you and outward to others. You cannot take yourselves as exceptions.

There is a purpose for each one of you. It is your own purpose and it is up to you to fulfill it, and it necessitates the full use of all your abilities—your mental abilities—and your intuitional abilities. You must demand the most of yourselves, for some of you will be involved later in asking others to demand the most of themselves and you must serve as examples. You *(Florence)* are meant to teach other classes, but you must develop you own abilities to do so.

You *(Vera)* are serving a purpose that you still do not understand. And a good purpose.

Now I speak to you when many conditions and many circumstances form together. This is independent of your time. You had better take advantage of it.

You *(Amelia F)* would do well to listen to him more. He *(Oliver F)* does not speak often of many matters in which he deeply believes. And because he does not speak of these, you do not realize that he has a full and varied innerlife. And that his thoughts go inward, though he does not speak of them.

I gave you *(Lydia)* messages when I said that I would and you received them.

Now, I do not want any of you drifting. You cannot afford to drift. You cannot afford to come here and see me as a fine old fellow either. For these characteristics by which you know me are but one portion of my personality and my reality. And I come to you from distances that you cannot evaluate.

Truths must be translated so that you can understand them. And I must appear to you, then, as a translation of what I am.

(Present at this class: Lydia, Sally, Brad, Vera, Amelia, Oliver, Florence and Theodore.)

ESP CLASS SESSION, SEPTEMBER 16, 1969
TUESDAY

(Matt Adams read three palms: Lydia, Florence, Rachel)

Now, I am here to welcome back a certain member of our group who had to leave the group for several reasons—and read me correctly in this particular instance where my friend Ruburt did not read me correctly *(addressed to Rachel).*

The time has indeed come, however, for you to return. Our Areofranz *(Matt)* read you quite well and that does indeed include the interpretation that he gave concerning your malady *(The malady: Rachel's ailing foot).*

There is some information that I want to give you, but I will not give it to you this evening. The information has to do with the nature of your own consciousness and with these personalities of which you have been speaking. There is some vital information that you do not have—information that has not been discussed in class, and it is time that you had it.

I also welcome our new student *(Mimi)* and, as always, my friend Areofranz. I welcome also our new bride *(Emma)*; I have looked in on you and I will have more to say to you tomorrow, and to you.

I will help each of you according to the extent to which you allow me to help you—and therein, indeed, lies a mighty tale. There are others ready to help you—again, when you are ready to permit their aid.

Now, I have been here all evening, and I shall be here until the door is closed. But I will not be speaking to you for that time.

I wanted you to know that I was here; but, more than that, I wanted you to know that you are ready for more information. But I am going to ask something of you this time. The days are finished when you can just listen.

I am going to give information that you can use and check out for yourselves. I want to tell you what you can do with your own consciousness and encourage you to use it. I do not expect you to jump ropes around your consciousness, but I do expect you to realize that you can use it in many ways. I do not expect you to play tricks with it, but I do hope you will realize that you can use it as a flashlight—that you can turn it in different directions.

There are different realities into which you can glimpse, and it is time for you all to look.

We will have journeys here, in class. I cannot trust some of you to work at home.

I have not forgotten that I told you I would give you a test. And, some evening, you *(Matt)* may read my palm. It will take some doing on my part, if not yours. But I will see that the palm is Jane's.

Now, it is good to see you all—I am glad to be jovial with you. I understand that Ruburt was not too jovial last week.

I enjoy being quiet and listening to your thoughts, which are like locusts. I will let our friend take back his class. In any case, he has told me that he is treating me like a goody in that he does not feel you appreciated our last session. And so he tells me I should only come through and give you my greeting. And so, I give you my greeting. I am kinder than he is.

There will be some more travel on your part *(Sue and Ned)*. And we would appreciate further cooperation this time. Houses are to be entered—astral houses, physical houses, thought-form houses—they are to be entered. Before I leave you, yes, I <u>am</u> conscious when I am not here. It is <u>Ruburt</u> who is in a Jane trance most of the time.

(Present: Rachel C, Matt and Emma Adams, Theodore and Vera, Lydia, Sue and Ned, Florence, Brad, Amelia, and Florence. Jane's list included Sally Benson and Mimi Ford.)

ESP CLASS SESSION, OCTOBER 14, 1969 TUESDAY

I do not approve of what has been said so far. And there are a few points I would like to make. You have not one, but many conscious selves. You have more than one conscious mind. What we want you to do is something quite different. We want you to change the channels of your awareness. We want you momentarily to stop using one of your conscious minds and learn how to tune into another one of your conscious minds.

In order to gain knowledge, in order to discover your reincarnation realities, you must not necessarily block out the conscious mind with which you are familiar and turn to sleep. Instead, you see, it is like turning off one channel and turning on another channel.

If you consider the conscious mind that you know as one door, this is the door through which you usually walk. You stand at the threshold of this door and look into physical reality. But there are other doors—you have

<u>other</u> conscious selves. These conscious selves are like windows that belong to your entire identity. When you look from one window, you look out into physical reality. When you look out through other windows, you look into other realities.

You are not expected to become unconscious. There is no need for you to feel that when you block out one conscious mind, there is only blankness—for you have other conscious minds. There are other conscious portions of your own personality. We simply want you to look out other windows. The shades are pulled down now over these other windows *(indicating the particular windows in the room)*. We simply want you to snap the shade open and look out. This can be a joyful and an alert experience. It does not need to have to do with sleep and relaxation as it has been spoken of in your recording. That recording, to some extent, maligns the subconscious and the inner self.

It is true that for a moment when you close one conscious door, the door with which you are familiar, there is an instant perhaps before you open another shade and use another portion of your conscious mind to look into other realities...and you may momentarily feel disorientation.

These other portions of your own consciousness are alert even in the sleep state. You may not have always been aware of these other conscious portions of yourself, but they are not vague. They are not vague. You may need to learn the methods by which you can perceive other realities ... simply because you are not used to manipulating these other conscious portions of yourself. But these portions are as critical and even as intellectual and as waking and as valid and as real as the consciousness with which you are ordinarily familiar.

What you perceive, using other portions of yourself, can be far more vivid than the reality in which you usually focus your attention. These other realities are not shadowy or dim. You must simply learn to use your inner eyesight—a different kind of eye—a different kind of vision.

It is true that some physical relaxation is of great benefit. It is true also that certain methods—and I have given some of these to you—are necessary to allow you to switch your focus of attention from physical reality to other realities. It is true, also, that it takes some training to use these other conscious portions of yourself. But remember that these other portions of your identity <u>are</u> portions of <u>your</u> identity—they are a <u>part of you</u>. Your perceptions can be vivid using them. There is no need for you to feel that any reincarnational information must come in a murky, shadowy way through vast areas of a self that you neither know nor understand. Memories of other childhoods can be fresh and bright. You can indeed feel a sense of recognition and familiarity.

You have ten fingers and you use them all. Yet, what you are saying is, "This finger is my conscious awareness and I will use it and I will not use these other nine—or if I use these other nine, I cannot use my conscious awareness." Your fingers are all fingers and these other portions of yourself are all conscious. They may not be conscious of each other. They may not be conscious of each other, but they are conscious. They are all part of your own identity. They are all portions of your abilities and personalities...that you are meant to use.

Other portions of your consciousness may have as much difficulty seeing through the windows as you do. You will find yourself, for example, looking through many of these windows at the same time. And in these windows you may view other portions of yourself. These portions may seem objective—distant from you—and different. You may seem to be viewing strangers. The viewpoint is entirely different form the viewpoint of any other figures, however. Do you follow me?

Now that I have pointed out what I do not like about the recording, if you still choose to go ahead with it, you may indeed, but I shall interrupt again if I do not like what you are listening to.

(Break.)

When you turn off what you think of as your conscious mind, then another conscious mind clicks into focus. You have more than one conscious mind. You can experience them only one at a time, although they exist simultaneously. When you cease using the conscious mind that you know, there is another one that will take over—you do not sink into a limbo. You are used to thinking of hypnosis in this following manner: You seem to think, most of you, that the conscious mind is blocked out, and then what follows is a murky and a shadowy version of the normal conscious mind—that the subconscious, for example, deals with material that you cannot understand consciously.

The facts are that when you close off the conscious mind that you know, another more alert conscious mind takes over; a conscious mind that belongs to you that has far more vision than the one you usually use; a conscious mind that is aware of more than you are usually aware of.

([Florence:] "Isn't this what the psychologists call the ego and the super ego and the subconscious... ?")

I am talking in terms of the self within the self within the self...the self that watches the self... the conscious alert self of which your present conscious mind is but a shadow. And this has nothing to do with the ego, which is only a small portion of waking consciousness.

(Break.

(Again Florence stated she felt that it might just be a matter of semantics.)

When your precious psychologists walk out of their bodies and tell me what is in California, then I will listen to their theories of personality <u>and</u> when your psychologists put on the type of personality performance that I can put on—then I will listen to them when they tell me about the ego and subconscious. When <u>their</u> theories are <u>broad enough</u> to explain telepathy and clairvoyance and out-of-body realities, then I will listen to them and to their theories. <u>Their</u> ego and <u>their</u> subconscious and <u>their</u> superego and <u>their</u> id leads them no further than a worm that wiggles in the grass and is dead forever tomorrow, and even the <u>worm</u> has more reality than they are willing to assign to one human consciousness.

And even, therefore, the worms dance in the grass and laugh at your psychologists' theories, for even they know that they are more than the reality the psychologists would grant to you. If you were what the psychologists think you are and no more then would you be faced with an extinction predestined for you before your birth.

No more than the atoms and molecules that compose you and as anonymous as the elements and even <u>they</u> whisper through the air. Do not tell me that my theory of personality is only another word for the ego or for your psychologists' theories.

(Break.)

Now. Theoretically, you can be aware of more than one consciousness at once. Practically speaking, you must close one door before you can open another. Then you can learn to have both open at the same time. What I objected to in your recording was the implication that once the conscious mind as you know it was quieted there was no other conscious mind to take over, and that the ordinary conscious mind was the only conscious mind that you have.

In comparison, you see, to the other conscious portions of your own personality, you are asleep. <u>I tell you to awaken</u>. This is not as Ruburt would say, to knock the ordinary conscious mind. It is merely to tell you that it has been adapted for one specific purpose in physical reality.

Now, you are an identity. Pretend that you hold a flashlight. The flashlight is your own consciousness. Now. You can turn this flashlight in an infinite number of directions. These directions are always available to you. But instead, you get the habit of directing your flashlight in one particular direction. You hold it in this direction constantly and you have forgotten, you see, that there are any other directions.

All you have to do is swing the flashlight in other directions. You must momentarily, for now, shift the focus of the flashlight. And when you shift it, the direction in which you are used to looking will momentarily appear dark, but other images and realities will become available to you. There is nothing to prevent you from swinging the flashlight back. And when you learn what you are doing, when you learn what you are doing—then you will learn how to hold the flashlight stationary and still illuminate all these other areas. And these whole other areas represent human personality and all its potentials.

Pretend, pretend that yourself...your whole identity, is a tape, such as being used here, but in stereophonic. Now, pretend that you have eight channels on this fantastic machine. Now, the whole self is composed, to use this analogy, of the entire eight channels. Usually, however, you can only play one channel at a time. The whole self, however, is aware of the entire eight channels and is able to keep track of them. The conscious mind as you know it is only one note on the first channel, not even the entire channel. You can learn methods that will enable you to tune in on these other channels. These other channels are all conscious portions of your own entire identity. They may or may not be aware of you as one small note on the first channel. They must learn to tune in, but many of them have already learned this knowledge and it is part of their own training.

What I want you to realize is that there is one entire fully alert and aware identity of which you are a part. As long as you are used to looking in only one direction, you will not be aware of this. But when you look, as with the flashlight, have faith that you will see.

([Class Member:] "Would we necessarily, in looking out of all these windows, see a visualization of another channel? Are we limited in our ordinary consciousness by what we think we might see and this would... ?")

You are indeed. And in many cases, the visualization in itself would be a distortion. However, you could examine the distortion. In many cases, without the distortion, you would see "nothing."

([Class Member:] "You might, instead, sense or feel something?")

Correct! The inner senses are the portion of you that can be used with confidence to perceive these other realities. Now you should reread the material on the inner senses and all of you should learn <u>what they are and how to use them!</u>

([Class Member:] "Are there any overlappings of these personalities? Our main focus is our conscious personality... these others of which we are unaware consciously, do they

become absorbed into us in time or are they always there but... ?")

I am not sure whether or not I correctly interpret your question. However, you only <u>seem</u> to be the main conscious part of your identity. Other portions of yourself may consider <u>their</u> selves as the main origin of personality. They would therefore look at you and at your ego, you see, as a fringe self. The ego seems to think that all other portions of the personality circle about it. This is hardly the case.

(*Break.*

(*Someone commented that we come back to do a sort of penance.*)

There is no penance! You are here to develop. You do learn the consequences of your thoughts and actions, and you face them. But there is no penance! And I tell you this: there is no guilt. And I tell you: there is no guilt. You learn the consequence of your action and you face the consequence of your action. You create the idea of guilt. And when you believe in guilt, then you create the penance in accordance to how strongly you believe in the guilt.

Now, we have a new rug. I can throw the glasses, and I know they will not break. Give us a moment. You have had your breathing spell. You will be with us for some time in the group, but you have changed your position within it *(addressed to Rachel).*

Now, the reincarnational information is available, not only on my part but on your own. And when you are ready, you will accept it from yourself and from me. When you are ready to accept it, you will already have worked through many problems that have stood in your way.

I have said this to you often, as a group; I say it [to] you again as a group, and I say it to you personally: <u>you form the physical reality that you know</u>. You form your daily life and your work situation. You make it, you choose it! Now, when you truly understand this, you can change it for the better, but until you really understand the truth behind my words, then you will look for excuses. Now you may partially be taken in by the excuses—Ruburt may be partially taken in by the excuses, <u>but I am not taken in by the excuses!</u> And an inner part of your own consciousness is not taken in by the excuses either!

I have told you this and I tell you again. You are amused when I rise to your friend's questions. You are amused by the very human characteristics I show. I make you laugh. But remember: The characteristics that I show to you, as I have told you often, are only a <u>small</u> portion of my reality. And I use them often as teaching tools. <u>and when you are ready to listen</u>, and when you can accept what I have to say without these characteristics, which you find so familiar and assuring, <u>then</u> your education may begin and Ruburt's also.

I appear to you—and I show myself to you—in certain ways—in familiar ways—so that you can sense the bonds between us that <u>do</u> exist. And yet, there are freedoms that have nothing to do with human consciousness as you understand it. There are roads that you will follow and you will look back on the selves that you know now as the first bare glimmerings of your birth.

And so when I speak to you, I speak to you often in sympathy and compassion that you know so little and have so far to go, and yet you travel a road that I have also traveled and so I can, to some extent, enter into your experience and understand reality as it now appears to you, and yet it is a limited and indeed a shadowy reality.

I will now bid you good evening. But before I go, let me say this: Ruburt does not let himself realize, as yet, what he knows. For right now he feels he cannot afford to. He is learning to operate in several realities at once. Now, in answer to a question that you asked earlier, I have spoken of this in the past—for a moment...

(The "other personality" interrupted at this point.)

[Seth II:] Let the human characteristics by which you know me, fade into their proper perspective. Seth as you know him, is distant in my own past, a reality that I scarcely remember. He is a portion of my reality and as such he continually exists. He does now exist in his own reality. Yet to me, all that is past. I am not only what he will one day become in your terms I am far more—and in me your Seth, while remaining a developing identity on his own, is a distant memory in my consciousness. We sent him to you in your terms in some indescribably distant past. He entered your universe in a reality I find difficult to remember. He gave guidance to your kind for eons of your time. I do not sufficiently understand the experience in which you are presently involved, in your terms.

We are involved in forming creations, realities, consciousness—worlds beyond your comprehension. Within these, Seth as you know him is a shadow within my awareness. Yet he is a part of what I was. There seems to be a dim connection between him and the Ruburt that you know.

We do not deal with sensory data, as you know it. We form the realities, we give birth to universes but within you now I can tell you is the breath of creativity—the source of All That Is of which you are a part..

(Seth.) Now, we will come to get our good friend back. He is lost in the netherlands. Give us a moment.

(Break.)

Now. You know Ruburt as Jane Butts. You have been given a demonstration of the steps through which consciousness may travel. You have been given a demonstration as to the directions in which you can flash your flashlight of consciousness and of the distant paths that this light can illuminate...

(The "other personality" took over, again, at this point.

(Seth II.) Do not imagine that we are not individuals or that because we seem alien to you that we do not know joy or creativity. Our joy forms universes. It is only because we are unused to bodies that communication is difficult. Our joy forms the universes that you know and dances through your molecules. Our consciousness gives fuel to your own. We possess the energy that gives your

sun light.

Your identity is like a sun that shines above you. You bask in it without knowing it is a part of your own identity.

I communicate through this body in your "now," and yet you do not realize the eons, in your terms, that pass even as this voice speaks. Your system has destroyed itself many times and has been reborn.

You each exist even in my "now" though you would not recognize the selves that you are. You will help create these realities of which I speak.

(Seth.) Now we will help little brother down and return him.

(Break.)

Now I wish you all a fond good evening, so you can all relax and not worry about our friend or about me vanishing in the superior mind of our superior friend. I can assure you that I have gone my own way as he has gone his own way—and the universes that I have had a hand in, have a far more emotional basis and I personally prefer them.

ESP CLASS SESSION, OCTOBER 21, 1969
TUESDAY

(The class was discussing the "other personality" (Seth II) when Seth entered the discussion.)

Now. He is not as scintillating as I am—but he has his reasons.

First of all, may I say good evening to you *(Rochelle K.)* and it is good to have you back *(Rose)* and I welcome you, and I welcome this one over here and I knew he *(Doug)* was coming.

Now despite my gentle, good-humored remarks about the personality you call Seth II, let me tell you something—You cannot translate the dimensions of his personality. What he is cannot be translated, in your terms.

His thoughts are not translated in those terms because you cannot rightfully call them thoughts in the way you are accustomed to thinking of thoughts. Now, a thought to him is a creative experience. What he thinks immediately <u>is</u>. It is not that he is cold, he has a different kind of thermal quality. He is <u>vast</u>. I am old, but he is <u>vast</u>.

Ruburt mentioned something earlier about a "Saturday afternoon." Unfortunately, <u>your world </u>would fit in one of his Saturday afternoons—if he knew what a Saturday afternoon was.

However, his energy is beyond <u>my</u> knowledge and his creativity is beyond my knowledge. I will not grow into what he is—we have our own ways to follow. And yet we are connected. And some of my energy, you see, also comes from him.

Now, I happen to like <u>my</u> worlds better. Otherwise, I would not come here so often. I have always dealt with emotion, but <u>he</u> deals with those realities that make emotions <u>possible</u>.

There is also a large effort made when he speaks through Ruburt and an effort on his part. He knows a portion of him is filtering down into this room. Now, when the sun shines and the rays fall from the sun down through your solar system, the sun is not consciously aware of its rays nor of the rooms that these rays may illuminate.

This "other personality" <u>is</u> aware that a part of himself is filtering down, and in his own way he is aware of you and of the room. But he is not aware of you as you know yourselves, and he is scarcely aware of me as I know myself. He is aware of me, but in another context, and in another dimension of existence.

I should tell you that I am sorry that I kept you so long last week. My friend Ruburt has been telling me that I must apologize. And I should tell you that I have deep sympathy—but your time is not my time. I do try to take it into consideration. And yet those issues that might bring me to you in a session, have nothing to do with time as you consider it. Now I will let you take a rest period, but I have not said good evening, and you can all be comfortable. Our friend will not be speaking to you this evening, and he is <u>not</u> a bogey man.

(Break.)

Now. When I write my own book, you will read it word by word...and so shall you all, ...and then, there will be tests. I will give you a quiz on every chapter, for <u>my</u> book will soon be written. Ruburt is worried that I will not know how to address myself to his precious public.

He broods over this. However, to begin with, Ruburt writes as Ruburt or, if you prefer, Ruburt writes as your friend Jane. Now, I can write as the many selves I have been, with full knowledge of my background so that I can address myself to mothers, and fathers, and children...consciously remembering my experience in those roles.

This book will be written from the inside out. And when I write the book, I will be thinking of the members of this class. For you are more representative than you know.

(To Brad) And where is my brandy? You tell me you are going to bring me this brandy and I have, instead, this wine!

(Brad said that he had brought it but he had not drunk it during a previous class.)

Ruburt would not let me take advantage of it because he does not like brandy, but if it were here!

(Brad replied that he would arrange to have brandy on hand every class night, and a cigar!)

Now, remember, try to keep two things in your mind. One: I am who I say I am and these characteristics of mine, are mine, insofar as they can be translated.

Remember also that I have one main role, and that role is that of a teacher. And, therefore, I use my characteristics as teaching aids.

You would not relate to me nearly as well if you did not think of me as a crotchety, endearing gentleman of genteel manner.

The "other personality" is more difficult to relate to, for he is naked of these characteristics. So shall you all one day be naked of these characteristics. Remember that! And remember also that even these characteristics of mine are put on again as a garment that was at one time discarded. The characteristics are mine, and I rejoice in them!

But they are the characteristics in your terms that were mine a long time ago, and I don them again as an old garment that is familiar and dear.

If you would travel within yourselves, you would find some subjective awareness, some glint of recognition, that would give you a hint of what I mean. As I have told you often, you have your own roads and it is up to you to explore them.

It is up to you to look for these signposts. Ruburt's personality is a walk *[warp handwritten in margin]*, in dimensions, but <u>your</u> personalities are also walks *[warps]* in dimensions... and you can look inward. You will find old friends, but you will find more than old friends and they will help you in your search.

All of you are a part of many times and many places. If you would put aside these selves that you take for granted, you could experience your own reality, your own multidimensional reality. These are not fine words that mean nothing. I do not harp to you about theory simply because I want you to spout theory, but because I want you to put these theories into practice for yourselves and discover the selves that are within you.

You will not be alone in your search. I have been around in a few of your endeavors *(Rochelle K.)*. These are not words signifying nothing. They are keys that you can use to your own advantage. There is a reality behind my words and this reality is yours—you have only to pursue it.

Now that I have gone on so jovially, I will let you rest.

(Break.

(There was a comment about Seth's statement, as to how he had been around in a few of Rochelle's endeavors. Seth clarified this.)

All I said was that I had been with you in many of your endeavors, when you were alone at home and when your inner self went traveling.

(Break. Brad stated his desire that Seth would more explicitly set forth the steps which we should follow. Seth interjected the following.)

First, you must understand the nature of what you call reality. To some very small extent, I have begun to explain this in the Seth material. The five hundred and some odd sessions we have, however, barely represent an outline—but they are enough to begin with.

The ideas themselves will start you thinking. Besides the outer senses that you take for granted, you have inner senses. These will enable you to perceive reality as it exists independently of the physical matter that you know. You must learn how to use, develop and recognize these inner senses. The methods are given in the material. But you cannot utilize the material until you understand it.

The material itself is cleverly—if you will forgive the term—cleverly executed so that as you grapple to understand it you are already beginning to use abilities beyond those that you take for granted.

You must first of all cease identifying yourself completely with your ego. You must not just listen to my words but realize not only that you are more than your ego, but that you can perceive more than your ego perceives. You demand more of yourself than you have ever demanded in your life.

This material is not for those who would deceive themselves with pretty, packaged, ribboned, truths—truths that are parceled out and cut apart so that you can digest them. That sort of material does serve a need, and there are many who give it and it is helpful for those who need it. This material demands more. It demands that you intellectually and intuitively expand—it demands that you use your abilities.

There are other ways—far more difficult, and you are not ready for those, but you are ready for the methods that I have given if you are willing to work. And yet by work, I mean a joyful endeavor, a spontaneous endeavor.

You have simply to allow yourselves to be yourselves.

When you were children, you knew you were a part of All That Is and you allowed your perception some freedom. That is all that I ask of you now!

Someone—I forgot who—once said, "unless you become like little children, you shall not enter the kingdom of heaven."

And, he was not speaking symbolically.

(Break. The class was discussing the apparent variations in appearance of Jane as Seth.)

Now there is something you do not understand, and so I will set you straight. It has been given in our material—I do not want to upset any of you. You have all seen, I suppose, educational TV. Now when you turn on your miraculous contrivance and you see the teacher on the screen, that does not mean that at that moment, the teacher is on the screen. Do you follow me? The teacher is quite legitimate but he is not there when you see him.

And so sometimes you are given a recording. Now this does not mean that I am not present in such sessions, anymore than it does not mean that the information you are given by the teacher, on the screen, is not legitimate. It is a reasonable facsimile.

Much of our work is done when Ruburt is sleeping... or when he is otherwise engaged. And he becomes then your vitalized TV set, and I am sorry that the reproduction is not as good as the original because I also have other endeavors and other places, in your terms, that I must be.

I do not mean to infer that our dear friend Ruburt is simply a channel on a TV screen. Now tonight I am here clearly. My total emotional immersion may be far away from your system, in your terms, when I know I am wanted here, therefore I can appear here. For the program has already been taped.

Now when your teacher appears on the TV screen, he is not aware consciously of himself within the image that you see. It is completely a taped production. When the same thing happens in our classes, however, I <u>am</u> here—but to a lesser extent than I am at this moment. I am aware of myself, going with our analogy, within the image that you would see on your TV screen.

Now. I am indeed here this evening with more energy and power than a facsimile. But this does not mean that I am not here on those other occasions when you hear me speak. Do you follow me? This has been given in our sessions and Ruburt and Joseph understand it.

Now you will have your fun trying to figure out whether we are having an original or a taped session.

(Break.)

Now I will not keep you because my friend is reminding me of your hour. However, we have a Dean and now we have a Doc. *(Addressed to Doug Dobbs and Lydia.)*

Now, you have been intrigued by your own experiences in the past. You felt, however, that those episodes which you experienced were intellectually stifling and did not allow you room to grow—they did not encourage curiosity or honest questioning.

They did not encourage you to use your own abilities and look within yourself. So now I encourage you to look within yourself and to use your abilities, both intuitional abilities and intellectual abilities.

Now you believe that you are using your intellectual abilities, but you have only begun to use them. You have not begun to use your intuitional abilities to anything like their true extent.

So I encourage you to use both. And you are welcome to our classes whenever you can attend.

I tell you to examine what you see and what you hear, not only here in this room and in these classes, but to examine what you see in physical reality in your normal life. The two of you can be of great benefit to each other, but only when you feel free to use your intellectual <u>and</u> intuitional abilities to their full—and do not fell hampered on either side.

Now I invite you all to close your eyes, to listen to my voice and to use it as a launching pad for your own experiences. You can travel where I am. Your self is not a closed door. The inner portion of you is open. You have senses which you have not been using, and I invite you now to use them. I invite you, therefore, to listen within yourself and to use my voice as a beacon in the darkness—a point of safety. It can illuminate many ways and you can feel safe to follow these ways into other personalities that are a portion of yourself—and into other realities in which you also have your existence.

Therefore I invite you to forget the bodies that you know, to set your inner selves free. I ask you, as Ruburt has often, to realize that within yourself there are endless dimensions, and that you can travel safely within them. I ask you to realize that your mind is a gateway into other dimensions. And I ask you to open your inner eyes, and I ask you to look around at the inner world in which you also have your existence. I ask you to sense within yourselves the energy in this voice that you hear, to realize that this energy is also a portion of your own energy—the energy of individuality, the energy of the universe, the energy that grows you from a fetus to the self that you know.

I ask you to realize that within yourself is the prime identity that gave birth to your own personalities...and within yourselves there are personalities that you have forgotten. There are personalities that you have not yet become; but you can see, you can see a pathway and you can travel through it.

You can use my voice as a light to illuminate those pathways of existence that are now clear to you.

As I have not been physical for some time, so you are not physical. You only inhabit a body and you presume that you are your body, but you are far more than the body that you know.

Then I invite you to open up within you those gateways of knowledge, those pathways of existence. I entreat you to find within yourselves echoes of this energy that now fills this voice and to use that energy to prepare you, to prepare you in the journey towards self-realization.

<u>You form this physical reality that you know</u>. You have formed your past lives. You will form your future lives, in your terms, but they exist simultaneously now in ultimate reality. Allow yourselves to feel the strength and vitality that is your own. Allow yourselves to recognize the energy of the universe as it flows through your still-physical frames.

Allow yourselves to listen to the inner voice, the inner voice that gives vitality and existence to the physical bodies that you know. Realize that there is a vitality and a reality behind my words and my voice that exist also in your own experience. And be brave enough to grab hold of this energy and this knowledge as your own.

And now I ask you to return to the room and to your images.

I ask you to open your eyes.

ESP CLASS SESSION, NOVEMBER 25, 1969
TUESDAY

(Attending were Sally, Rose, Rachel, Amelia and Brad.)
Now I have a few brief remarks and then my friend Ruburt wants to send our friend Rachel here back through time to another reincarnation.

The remarks are these—We will and we have, to a very small extent here, begun a study of multidimensional psychology...and it will be the psychology of the future for it will regard personality in its true and entire light. Methods will be given that will allow the present ego, to some extent, to become aware of its own greater reality. And a man or a woman who is aware of only one of his or her own egos will be considered an idiot, indeed. But this will take some time.

Now, this is a quiet evening and I am pleased with our small gathering. I wanted to tell you that symbolically, you *(Brad)* are winning, you are making adjustments, in more than weight. For the weight was indeed symbolic. You will find that some further adjustments will be much easier. The inner adjustments came first and the loss of weight later. The loss of weight is a physical materialization of the inner change. And you can expect others to follow.

Now you may or may not realize that here we have made a small, a very small, start in the study of <u>multidimensional personality</u>. And the theories are not yet fully presented by any means. But the theories will be laid out, and clearly, and the methods will be laid out, and clearly. And I hope that by the time these theories are laid out, you can use them well. And you are beginning to use them now whether or not you realize it. For you cannot understand the self that you know when you think that it is the only self that you are. For the self that you know is only a small portion of your entire identity.

And Jung's so-called "unconscious" is very conscious indeed. When you allow yourselves enough freedom, you will be able to close your eyes and become aware of these other fully conscious portions of your own identity. For when you momentarily leave aside your ego, as I have told you before, there is not chaos, there is not darkness, there is not a maze of subjectivity. Instead, there is a fully conscious and wise light. And the light belongs to other layers of your own personality. It illuminates your own egotistical awareness even now whether or not you realize it, and it guides your actions even now whether or not you realize it.

And do not judge according to your egotistical ideas alone. I am speaking to you now since you have set yourself *(Brad)* some problems. It took courage to set yourself the particular problems that you did for this existence, otherwise you would have tackled so many at one time, so to speak. There were certain truths that you found difficult to face. Now when I say this, I do not mean that the truths were difficult. I merely mean that in past lives there were certain portions of reality in which you did not have experience. And in this life you decided to experience these. And you are so doing and you are working toward solutions. If you knew this and if you knew what the problems were at this point, the problems would not be as real and the solutions would not be as valid. It would be like cheating in an examination.

I wanted to know that I was present here this evening and that I have been listening to your conversation.

(Break.)

...It means that the personality exists in many

dimensions at once. Now this includes not only reincarnational material in your terms, but the realization that the personality in the dream state is actually as alert and conscious as it is in the waking state. Now pretend for a moment that you are your dreaming self. And you want to understand the nature of physical reality. So you must peek out at physical reality, while the body sleeps and the eyes are closed and the senses are "dimmed" in your terms. You would gain little information, and yet you are in the same position attempting to understand the nature of the dreaming state with your waking consciousness.

Now. I have told you often that there are methods by which you can indeed take your waking self into the dream state and follow your own travels. Now you follow them but you *(Rose)* will not remember; and you *(Sally)* follow them sometimes; and you *(Rachel)* follow them sometimes; and you *(Amelia)* are beginning to put one foot upon the path; and you *(Brad)* have not as yet allowed yourself to remember any of your dream encounters. But the point is that you can indeed learn to do this—that it is not impossible. It is not only probable, but it is not even difficult.

Once psychology realizes that the personality is also alert and conscious in the dream state, then indeed its precepts and its bases must change. For information is given to you not only in your waking, conscious, alert daily life but in what you would call your unconscious sleep state. Now your sleeping self is awake all of the time—you dream all of the time. Your dream life is continuous, only your waking ego closes out the inner stimuli and does not see it, for it must concentrate upon physical daily reality. But it can learn to look inward, change the focus of its awareness and take quick pictures of this inner environment. So more than reincarnational existences are involved.

I do not need sweaters—I have no body to put one on *(to Rachel knitting a sweater)*.

You *(Rachel)* are somewhat like Ruburt, in that you are gifted but you are also highly cautious. You know very well that you are gifted. You are concentrating upon your job and upon physical security, and you are determined that you will be well cared for in your later years. All your conscious efforts are focused in that direction. And at the present time you are not willing to give that much attention to these other portions of your personality that you recognize do exist. And you have recognized your own gifts for some time. You are much more aware of your inner travels than you think you are. You know more about your nightly excursions than you admit to yourself. You come to class because you like me—you also come to class because it is your contact with this inner reality and you do not want to lose contact with it. You are not willing, however, to go all the way, at this point. You can, however, allow yourself more freedom than you are now allowing yourself. And I tell you this honestly—you can afford yourself more freedom than you are presently allowing yourself. You are afraid for example that in psychological time—granted you find the physical time for it—you will take needed energy away from your physical pursuits. Now I tell you, you are overly concerned with these pursuits, that you could get the same results by trying less, by being freer. You are trying too hard... you can get better results by being freer—in your relationships with those with whom you work and in your own attitude—you will get better physical results. You will also get better physical results if you will allow yourself more inner freedom for you will gain energy and strength that you need now. You will not be depleted, but refreshed.

Also, there is an old relationship here going back some many centuries and not of an important nature. But there was an acquaintanceship when you knew each other and you realized this.

(Break.)

Now. For now, since I do not have brandy, I will drink wine.

([Brad:] "My wife took the brandy that I had for you, hard though that may be to believe.")

I have heard many excuses in my life... ! ! !

Now we will start with you. If you have any questions, you may ask them.

([Rachel:] "You have taken me by surprise.")

The best questions come when you are taken by surprise, they are the ones that mean the most. *(Long pause.)*

Give me a moment first while you are thinking.

There is a friend of yours who does not have too much time here. Now I am speaking comparatively and am not giving you times and dates. This is a male. It is a strange relationship you had, for he was an uncle of yours in a past life. And there are undercurrents that still remain. The undercurrents are important—they make sense of a relationship that otherwise would make you question it—for why do you like this person so much, you see? And he was a beloved uncle. Now there seems to be another younger man connected perhaps with one of your daughters, who may be offered either a new job or something new in his line of work that may tax him and yet he will feel that he must accept it—for he is driven by ambition—and he will accept it. There is also a younger woman close to you and with her there will be an entirely new turn, a change of lifestyle.

Your husband, incidentally, in this life has no regrets. There seems to be in his memory an affair—the two of you in a car, after a party many years ago. I am not sure of names here, so there may be a distortion, but the name "Estelle" seems somehow in the background, as if Estelle gave a party or was involved with it—that you attended. Not someone close to you. After the party there seems to have been an argument between you and your husband—and something to do with a lamp. I hope—I hope you did not hit him with it.

Now his attitude toward you is one of humorous affection. Give us time here. He also believes you are overextending yourself in trying too hard. You are naturally, regardless of what you think, a good business woman. And you can use your psychic abilities in that line. But when you become overconcerned, consciously, then you hamper good results.

Do not become bored and think that I have no regard for you *(Amelia)* because I am speaking to our older class members, for you are coming along well with your own progression and your dream memories will get much better.

Now what are your questions?

([Rachel:] "I cannot fathom how I am overextending myself.")

You are overextending your energies by an overconcern. You are well equipped to handle yourself financially and in the business world, but your fear that you cannot do so is making you try too hard for something that should and can come easily.

([Rachel:] "Seth, why can't I remember my dreams?")

Because you try too hard when you try, because you do not relax enough and because you have this compulsive idea of getting along financially. And you are afraid in your terms of taking energy away from these pursuits. Now, your psychic abilities can help you in your daily life if you will let them do so. You are afraid to let yourself go in those terms. You want very much to have your feet solidly in physical reality, and you are afraid that if you let yourself go you will miss your footing, and this is not the case.

([Rachel:] "What am I trying to prove in this reincarnation?")

Now, you see, you have come up with a question. And in one of our class sessions, we will answer it thoroughly. We cannot answer it thoroughly this evening. There is a motive behind it, and unless I miss my guess you will discover what the motive is. And you are already beginning to discover what the motive is. Now. Give me a moment.

(Long pause.)

Try your psychological time experiments. Use the image of the fire. It is your symbol of knowledge, and you can trust where it leads you. That scene is very vivid now, and it is important to you.

Now. What is your question? *(Brad).*

([Brad:] "In many ways my relationship with my wife has been destructive. I am now at a crossroads where I could end this relationship. However, I feel a strong relationship with her, perhaps a karmic relationship—something I must solve with her in this life. ")

Now. There is not a karmic relationship with her. She stands in your mind for someone else with whom you did have a karmic relationship. That is not, however, your main problem. You have attempted in many ways to set up a strong relationship with your environment. You have tried to do this through weight. You have tried to say, "I am here solidly. *(Pause.)* Look at me. Who is more real than I for I take up so many inches of space? I weigh so much, I am here." At the same time, you were afraid of physical reality, and because of your environment in this life, you are afraid that you could not deal with it. You must first prove to yourself that you can indeed deal with it.

([Brad:] "Am I succeeding at all?")

You are barely beginning to do so. Now. Your wife has not been the symbol of a female to you, but of a male. Ruburt has told you this. You are now beginning to approach the point where you feel you can hold your own in physical reality.

([Brad:] "How vital is she to me?")

She was vital to you as a symbol but not a symbol of independence, but as a symbol of dependence. And neither of you would have agreed to the separation nor would the separation have taken place until both of you realized that it was time for this event to occur.

([Brad:] "Are you implying it is ended for—"

I am implying that it is now the time for you to become independent, that you know this and that she also knew it.

([Brad:] "Could a new relationship with her exist with me as the dominant?")

I did not say "dominant" nor did I imply a relationship of dominancy in those terms. I am speaking of a relationship whereby you as an individual know you can hold your own in physical reality. This does not, therefore, imply a position of dominancy.

([Brad:] "Do I need her? I want her. The dilemma has immobilized me.")

This is a natural situation. However, the situation is a <u>cover</u> over the initial problem. And you will get nowhere—either in the relationship or without it—until you assert yourself in relation to your environment and realize that you are strong enough on your own to survive in physical reality. This is the problem that has been shielded behind the relationship. It is your <u>fear</u> that you could not survive that made you cling to the relationship. And it is still that fear that would make you want to continue it.

As to the relationship with you and your wife, it has changed—it may change for the better if you use the opportunity.

([Brad:] "Do you mean then that we will go back together?")

That is a possibility, but if it occurs, it will no longer be the same relationship—and it should not be, and must not be, your main concern—for it is a shield for the deeper problem.

For many reasons having to do with your own past existence, and with your mother in this life, there was a basic insecurity and a feeling that you were not strong enough to survive on your own. This is what you must solve, and you are now ready to solve it, or the relationship between you and your wife would not have reached this point.

(Break. Jane asked during break what transpired. Brad said that it dealt with his struggle with reality—and his having to "face the music." Seth interjected the following:)

Now. The interpretation is not quite correct. For one thing, this still involves you with problems from a past life. In the episode that we mentioned earlier, and the famine, you are afraid that you could not cope with physical reality. The particular life that we dealt with so briefly made an extremely strong psychic effect upon you for it was nearly impossible to cope, there was no food. At that point in your lifetimes you had no skills. You were not equipped, because of your background, to cope with hard reality. Many others were in the same condition. But it left you, that life, with the feeling that physical reality was so difficult that you could not handle it alone. You resolved, therefore, to store up what food you had in terms of fat and protein to hold you against times of famine.

Consciously you knew this was a rich country in your present life, but unconsciously you held to these old feelings of fear. Now these old feelings also hung over you in that you felt that existence was much more difficult than it actually is now, and you are still relating to this old existence where times were so difficult. Now in that time, you definitely needed—and you had—someone to help you. In that life, in that life of which I am speaking—you had a man, roughly resembling your wife in bone structure, and in temperament. This man was not a family relationship...was not in a family relationship. He befriended you; you depended upon him. You have projected this upon your wife. The man was the kind who gained feelings of superiority and pleasure from helping you, but also helped you quite legitimately and kindly. When you found this sort of a woman in this life, for your own reasons, you were attracted to her. Now she, for quite other reasons, was attracted to you, but you have been terrified that alone you could not make it and would not survive.

Now. These feelings have been buried in your psyche, and they are no more legitimate than are the feelings concerning your weight that we have dealt with. You can and will survive. Now in the past existence, you were younger than this older man and you were constantly trying to prove to him that you could do without him, and so you are constantly trying to prove to your wife that you can do without her in that particular respect. And you can. But you are afraid that you could not. This put a strain on the relationship on your part but she also put strains upon the relationship that we shall not go into this evening, for her own reasons.

([Brad:] "Even though I may find I can get along without her, I think I will still feel I need her.")

You <u>may</u>, but the point is, you must know that the tree in the forest survives, and it reaches toward the sun. And you as an individual can survive, and then you are free to make other relationships—and in a wholesome and constructive manner. You must feel your oneness and your safety with the physical reality that you know. You must realize that you are projecting these insecurities from a past existence when you were indeed frightfully insecure. Therefore, you made demands upon this woman that she could not fulfill and she resented them. Now. She also made demands upon <u>you</u>, for her own reasons and we shall try to go into this some evening.

But you will find that it is easy for you to support

yourself, to find in other words a position and to hold it well, when you realize that these fears are projections from another time that have no relationship to the environment in which you now find yourself.

Now. Consciously—before this evening—you thought and you told yourself you could hold a position but you could not. If you were able to do so you would have done so. The tie-up between the past existence and the present one will affect you the same way in this case as it did in the case of your weight. Before you were indulging in wishful thinking. Now you should have the purpose and the inner realization that you can indeed achieve this regardless of your environment.

THE SETH AUDIO COLLECTION

THE LATER SETH CLASS SESSIONS (1972-79) are not included in The Early Class Session books and are available on CD along with transcripts. These are audio CD's of the actual Seth sessions recorded by Jane's student, Rick Stack, during Jane's classes in Elmira, New York, starting in 1972. Volume I, described below, is a collection of some of the best of Seth's comments gleaned from over 120 of the later Seth Class Sessions. Additional later Seth Class Sessions are available as The Individual Seth Class Session CD's. **For information ask for our free catalogue or visit us online at www.sethcenter.com .**

Volume I of The Seth Audio Collection consists of six (1-hour) cassettes plus a 34-page booklet of Seth transcripts. Topics covered in Volume I include:
- Creating your own reality – How to free yourself from limiting beliefs and create the life you want, • Dreams and out-of-body experiences. • Reincarnation and Simultaneous Time.
- Connecting with your inner self. • Spontaneity–Letting yourself go with the flow of your being. • Creating abundance in every area of your life. • Parallel (probable) universes and exploring other dimensions of reality. • Spiritual healing, how to handle emotions, overcoming depression and much more.

ORDER INFORMATION:
The Seth Audio Collection Volume I. Send name and address, with a check or money order payable to New Awareness Network, Inc. for $60 (Tapes), or $70 (CD's) plus shipping charges. United States residents in New York State must add sales tax. Shipping charges: U.S.—$7.00, Canada—$8, Anywhere in world -$15 (Slow) $24 (Fast)

New Awareness Network, P.O. Box 192, Manhasset, NY 11030
(516) 869-9108 between 9:00-5:00 p.m. Monday-Friday EST

Internet Orders and Info   **www.sethcenter.com**

Books by Jane Roberts from Amber-Allen Publishing

Seth Speaks: The Eternal Validity of the Soul. This essential guide to conscious living clearly and powerfully articulates the furthest reaches of human potential, and the concept that each of us creates our own reality.

The Nature of Personal Reality*: Specific, Practical Techniques for Solving Everyday Problems and Enriching the Life You Know..* In this perennial bestseller, Seth challenges our assumptions about the nature of reality and stresses the individual's capacity for conscious action.

The Individual and the Nature of Mass Events. Seth explores the connection between personal beliefs and world events, how our realities merge and combine "to form mass reactions such as the overthrow of governments, the birth of a new religion, wars, epidemics, earthquakes, and new periods of art, architecture, and technology."

The Magical Approach*: Seth Speaks About the Art of Creative Living.* Seth reveals the true, magical nature of our deepest levels of being, and explains how to live our lives spontaneously, creatively, and according to our own natural rhythms.

The Oversoul Seven Trilogy *(The Education of Oversoul Seven, The Further Education of Oversoul Seven, Oversoul Seven and the Museum of Time).* Inspired by Jane's own experiences with the Seth Material, the adventures of Oversoul Seven are an intriguing fantasy, a mind-altering exploration of our inner being, and a vibrant celebration of life.

The Nature of the Psyche. Seth reveals a startling new concept of self, answering questions about the inner reality that exists apart from time, the origins and powers of dreams, human sexuality, and how we choose our physical death.

The "Unknown" Reality*, Volumes One and Two.* Seth reveals the multidimensional nature of the human soul, the dazzling labyrinths of unseen probabilities involved in any decision, and how probable realities combine to create the waking life we know.

Dreams, "Evolution," and Value Fulfillment*, Volumes One and Two.* Seth discusses the material world as an ongoing self-creation—the product of a conscious, self-aware and thoroughly animate universe, where virtually every possibility not only exists, but is constantly encouraged to achieve its highest potential.

The Way Toward Health. Woven through the poignant story of Jane Roberts' final days are Seth's teachings about self-healing and the mind's effect upon physical health.

Available in bookstores everywhere.

Printed in the United States
207234BV00002B/1-120/P

9 780976 897859